For those from any country
who suffered injury
or the loss of life, limb, spirit, or loved one
in the Vietnam War.

the box

a memoir

lynne lorine ludwick

Lynne L. Ludwick

ISBN-13: 978-1943624003
ISBN-10: 1943624003
Published by Lockwood & Ludwick
Author contact: lynneludwick@yahoo.com
Available from amazon.com, createspace.com, and other retail outlets.

Preface

A Viet Cong veteran gave me a gift. I've never met him and I don't know his name, but his gift is the inspiration for this book. A good friend, Jim Petersen, was in the village of Hoc Mon, Vietnam when he encountered this man and learned his story. From Jim, I learned his approximate age, where he was raised, some of his wartime experiences and losses, and that he shed tears in the telling. I have shared what I know of his story by weaving it into some history of Vietnam and into my memories of growing up with my uncle, Eddy, whose life path had crossed with his. I have taken the liberty to base this veteran's feelings and perceptions on what I knew of him and also, as I reviewed Vietnam history, on what I discovered about the way many young Vietnamese felt in the 1960s when they joined with the Viet Cong. If you might know this Viet Cong veteran who sent me the gift in this box, please send me his name, so that I can personally thank him. Should that never happen, this book is my thank you to this man who reached out to a stranger linked by war.

I'm not an expert in either Vietnam history or American history and this memoir is not meant to be a history book; however, a minimal amount of historical information was necessary for the setting. The resources I used are listed in the back and can be accessed for additional historical information. My memories of events and conversations, as well as those told to me by others, are to the best of our recollections.

One name has been changed to honor the request for privacy.

Acknowledgements

This memoir would not have been written had it not been for two events which took place more than thirty years after the end of the Vietnam War. The first is when Andy Wahrenbrock had the courage to face the past by reaching out to my family in 2008. The second is when Jim Petersen, who took a trip to Vietnam in 2009, returned with a gift for me from a Viet Cong veteran. For these events, I thank Andy, Jim and the Viet Cong veteran, whose act of forgiveness inspired me to tell the story.

Many people have assisted in bringing this memoir alive and I thank them for sharing their stories. In addition to my memories, I've included those of my sisters, Judy McPhail and Karen Allen, and my brother Arthur Ludwick; my cousins Linda Lewis and John Schultz; my aunts and uncles, Sandy and Sal Melendez, and Gary and Jeanie Schultz. I've included memories of various others: Tom St. John, Chuck Duveneck, Warren Hansen, Steve Boyle, Dave Stafford, and some members of the 2nd Platoon, Charlie Company, 2nd Battalion, 12th Infantry, 25th Infantry Division of the U.S. Army, including Andy Wahrenbrock, Jerry Counts, Jerry Miller and Dave Glass. I am also grateful to Maryanne (her name has been changed to protect her privacy), for sharing her stories. Without the input from these people, this would have been half a story.

For their editing, fact-checking, and advice I would also like to thank my good friend, writer and editor Susan Stewart, my daughters Lindsey Lau and Lauren

Christophel, my sisters, Judy McPail and Karen Allen, my daughter-in-law, Whitney Higgins, my son, Michael Higgins, my friend, Patsy West, and my aunt, Sandy Melendez. A special thank you to Andy Wahrenbrock for sharing his Vietnam experiences and editing the war scenes ensuring that I depict them as accurately as possible.

For their artistic talent in designing the book cover I thank my sister and my daughter, Judy McPhail and Lauren Christophel.

I would also like to thank Chuck Bowlby, for being a support when I felt overwhelmed. I'd like to extend an additional thank you to my sister, Judy McPhail, and my daughters, Lindsey Lau and Lauren Christophel, for helping me with technology, and to Lindsey for encouraging me to begin this project and to Lauren for urging me to complete it. A special thanks to a fellow high school classmate, Ricky Ortner, who was in the United States Army infantry and "walked point" (the soldier in front) on nearly every mission his platoon took into the jungles of Vietnam. Ricky continually encouraged and urged me to finish this story for the sake of all who suffered in that war.

There is perhaps no better demonstration
of the folly of human conceits
than this distant image of our tiny world.

—Carl Sagan, American astronomer

Eddy, at five and me, at two.

Contents

Prologue   1
Chapter 1   Erma   3
Chapter 2   French Occupation   6
Chapter 3   The Farm   8
Chapter 4   Geneva Conference   17
Chapter 5   The Barn   20
Chapter 6   Viet Cong   44
Chapter 7   Future Farmer   46
Chapter 8   Diêm   58
Chapter 9   Graduation   60
Chapter 10   Fellow Comrade   75
Chapter 11   Anti-War Protests   77
Chapter 12   The War   92
Chapter 13   Cookies   105
Chapter 14   Tet   108
Chapter 15   A Sinister Plot   109
Chapter 16   War Continues   112
Chapter 17   Search and Destroy   113
Chapter 18   Tan Hoa   119
Chapter 19   Hoc Mon   126
Chapter 20   The Boy's Village   129
Chapter 21   Two Worlds Collide   131
Chapter 22   The Telegram   134
Chapter 23   Forty Years Later   142
Chapter 24   The War Ends   150
Chapter 25   The Box   151
Chapter 26   On the Bank of Stenner Creek   156
In Remembrance   163
Resources   164
Charities   165

the box

Prologue

The country is fresh, like rebirth after a forest fire. The war ended more than thirty years ago. Devastation remains only in the souls of those old enough to remember. A weathered Viet Cong veteran who rests in the sun remembers. Long-buried scars in his heart match wrinkles that run deep on his dark, finely featured face. He pleasures in little things in the post-war life and is enjoying a cup of lotus tea with his life-long friends and fellow veterans whose lives were spared. There were times he wished he'd died, had not suffered the losses. He has lived in this village his entire life. It's a day with blue sky and white, billowy clouds, which he cherishes, after the many years of the black and red of napalm. Children were born into napalm skies, thinking fire was as normal as rain clouds. He's surprised by a government car pulling into their village. He watches the first man emerge from the car and soon all are out, stretching their legs as if their trip has been long. The government men are well-dressed, in suits, and are as out of place here as a weed in a rice field. There is a stranger accompanying them, who is much taller than they, standing like a rubber tree among shrubs; he is blonde and light skinned. He has a few wrinkles like an older man but carries youth in his demeanor. The elderly Viet Cong veteran watches them wander the village, and watches other villagers begin to follow them. Soon, he eases himself off his wooden bench to find out what brings them to Hoc Mon.

California

2010

UPS left the package on my front porch; I had waited over a year for it. I carried it into the house and set it on my dining room table with a sigh of satisfaction knowing it had arrived safely, feeling the way I did when my babies were born healthy with all of their fingers and toes. It required a slow, deliberate, ceremonious opening, considering its contents. After cutting open the outer mailing box and removing the bubble wrap, I found a metal box nestled inside. Given the magnitude of its meaning, I reflected on its tiny size. I lifted it, noting a dragon and oriental characters embossed on the lid, and a neatly tied red ribbon wrapped around it like a Christmas gift. I held it to my heart and contemplated its journey from across the world, from hands in one country to hands in another, and I knew that inside the darkness of this box was a story to be told: a story of hatred, death and grief but also of love, life and healing. A story that whispered its message across time.

Chapter One
Erma

California
1945

The year before Eddy was born, his sixteen year old sister was killed. It was after midnight, in the earliest hour of Easter, April 1st, 1945, in the small town of San Luis Obispo where we were later born. It's a town nestled within a circle of hills which seem to protect and comfort it as if the earth rose up to do just that. My mother, Lorine, was their older sister, who was nineteen that night while she waited with a friend at the plain, unpretentious train depot, which rested along the bottom edge of one of the smaller hills. They were pacing and on edge, waiting for a friend on the delayed southbound train, wondering if it would ever come. Finally, the station master announced, "An accident has caused the delay, but I'm happy to report passenger train 72 will arrive shortly and all passengers are safe." The girls sighed, worry lifted, but not for long because the station master added, "We're looking for Lorine Schultz. If you're here please come to the office." My mother, shocked to hear her name, trembled, as if with premonition, and scurried into the station with her friend trailing.

The station master looked sadly at my mom and said, "Your father called, knowing you were here. I'm sorry to inform you that your sister was in the accident. This sergeant is here to escort you to join your parents at the scene." My mother's knees weakened as she was escorted to the police car.

Erma Elaine Schultz was the sister Eddy never knew, the aunt I never knew and the sister my mother never forgot. Erma had been babysitting for some young partiers. She was driven home by a twenty-two-year-old soldier stationed at Camp Roberts. A young mother of two toddlers had been in the passenger seat. The young, drunk soldier raced his '44 Ford sedan around two cars that were waiting at the railroad crossing on Palm Street, a crossing that doesn't exist now due to this accident. He sped over the tracks in the face of the approaching train. With no time to brake, the train slammed into them and pushed, twisted and battered the car a block further along the tracks until it finally fell off the overpass to Monterey Street, "pulverizing it," according to the newspaper. When my uncles, Gary, twelve, and Carl, eighteen, woke up that Easter morning, they were told their sister had been killed during the night. Their other sister, Sandy, just five months old, was too young to know the difference.

I have a photograph of Erma at eleven that I look at sometimes and wonder who she was, and whether she knew she was going to die only five years later. It was taken at the San Francisco World's Fair in 1939. She has black hair, straight and cropped at chin length. A pure, round face, with large, knowing eyes. My mother is in the picture too, as well as my grandfather, who, in that picture looks to me like a more handsome version of Prince Charles. In fact, he was a lineal descendent of kings, beginning with William the Conqueror. My mother was only fourteen in the picture, but wearing a skirt and jacket, looking much like an actress in a '40s film. My mother lost her sister due to a drunk driver, and the loss trickled down through time the way a stone might tumble down a river, affecting even her unborn offspring and in time, their offspring. I grew up with my mother's stories of Erma and also her fear of cars, trains, and loss, which, in turn, became mine.

Chapter Two
French Occupation

The Viet Cong veteran was born into a grieving country. At the time of his birth, millions of Vietnamese were dying of starvation. It was the time of WW II and the Japanese invasion. This baby was a survivor during the worst of times, but the worst of times seemed to have no end. The tiny S-shaped country of Vietnam, its size only 128,000 square miles, was ruled by various Chinese Dynasties for a thousand years, then finally ruled itself through various Vietnamese Dynasties from 938 A.D. until 1858 when Napoleon's French soldiers invaded. It remained occupied by France for nearly a hundred years until the Japanese invaded in 1940. He was a baby in 1945 when the Japanese were defeated at the close of WW II and the French reclaimed Vietnam, mainly for the profits from rubber trees. The people of Vietnam had independence in their hearts and on their minds so they didn't let the French take over without a fight. The Liberation Front of South Vietnam wanted peace, wanted the French out, and wanted to be free to rule their own country. This led to a revolt against the French in August 1945. The Vietnamese came out of their bamboo huts and crowded into the streets in protest; however, the French were not easily overtaken. They shot into the crowds, killing, arresting and torturing many, when this boy was a

*toddler. His first sights were of bloodshed, chaos and fear.
Yet he survived.*

Chapter Three
The Farm

California
1946–1955

Edward August Schultz was born into a grieving family. It was October 8th, 1946, just a year and a half after Erma's death. One might think my grandparents, Sam and Cornelia, made this new baby to replace their dear Erma and that may be true, but the way Grandma told me, since their three oldest children were so much older (twenty-one, nineteen, and fourteen), it was because they wanted a playmate for Sandy, who was almost two when Eddy was born.

My grandparents lived on a farm near California Polytechnic State University, more commonly referred to as Cal Poly, and they could see the lights and hear the cheering crowd during Friday night football games. At two, when Eddy heard the cheering, he would throw up his arms and holler, "Whoopee! We want a touchdown!" getting chuckles from his older siblings. When he was three years and twelve days old, I was born, the first of many who would make him an uncle. Ten months later my cousin, John, was born, and a few months after that, my sister, then John's brother, and it kept going like that for several years.

What my grandparents didn't anticipate was that their last two children gave me, their first grandchild, two playmates, Sandy and Eddy, which made going to

Grandma and Grandpa's farm my favorite place to go. Some of my earliest memories are the excitement I felt when we headed north from town on Santa Rosa Street and got in the right lane to go straight instead of the left lane to turn onto Foothill toward home. It meant we were going to Grandma's, which was as thrilling as if we were heading to Disneyland. Going to Grandma's meant cows, chickens, horses, riding the go-cart, swimming, and lots of play time because Sandy and Eddy were there.

Much of my childhood was spent at their farm. My mother and grandmother were both raising young children so it was natural for them to spend a lot of time together. My mother was in her mid-twenties and gave up her secretarial job to become a homemaker when I was born. She had married my dad, Art Ludwick, at twenty-one. When I was two and my sister, Judy, was one, my brother, Arthur, was born. My mom liked to tell that she had three kids under three. At two, since I was the oldest, I was her helper. Maybe that's why I enjoyed Sandy and Eddy so much; I didn't *always* have to be the oldest. When I was with them I was one of the younger kids. Since my grandmother was also a stay-at-home mom in her mid-forties with two young children, and she didn't drive, she relied on my mom to take her on errands and the weekly grocery shopping at a tiny market called Ellsworth's. These trips meant Sandy, Eddy, me, Judy and Arthur playing in the car while they bought groceries. When they came out they gave us each a turn, one at a time, to go into the store to pick a treat and this felt as special to me as if they'd said, "go pick a diamond ring."

Sometimes I visit where the farm was. In 2011, I stood in a parking lot where there had once been a circular dirt drive-way. I was staring at a college student housing complex called Stenner Glenn, named after the creek that meandered along the edge of the property. Thousands of students have lived there in the past thirty years, but for many years before, only one family lived on the four acres that was their farm. I wasn't seeing what was in front of me. Instead, I was seeing what once was. Only a trace of that time is left—the eucalyptus trees lining the bank of Stenner Creek and one avocado tree, a survivor, with cells within its bark that may have recorded events from long ago. Like perhaps the time when Eddy, at ten, climbed into its branches to collect avocados, then fell to the ground, breaking his arm. Thanks to my great uncle, Bill, that avocado tree is still standing and didn't turn to dust like everything else. It was dying seventy years ago and he told Grandpa it needed iron. So Grandpa pounded iron nails into the trunk, and today the tree, a survivor, proudly guards over the student parking lot.

Under the eucalyptus trees, though covered by fifty years of growth and dirt, there's an area where my grandparents threw their trash over the bank (this sounds terrible now, but it was a common occurrence on farms in their era and they had both grown up on farms). I'm tempted to do my own archeological dig to find artifacts from life on the farm. Maybe I would find one of the toy metal cars we played with under the shade of those trees.

I felt like a fixture, motionless, staring into the past, as time melted away. I witnessed it as vividly as if on a movie screen. It was like time-travel and the moment had a spiritual resonance as I wondered about time or the absence of time, thinking time might be vertical, not horizontal. Where did it all go? How could it have gone away? And how did it go so fast?

The white farmhouse, built in the early 1900s, focuses into view. The orange trees, majestic, and as tall and as full as the house, stand guard over the lawn just outside the back door. The eucalyptus trees whisper from the breeze and shade us as we play in the dirt. The sky is a clear blue with thin, white, wispy clouds gliding along with purpose. The bell from Cal Poly's clock tower rings, announcing the hour. The train shakes the earth as it speeds past.

"No, you can't use that stick for a car," Eddy says. Fantasy has its limits as far as he is concerned. His striped T-shirt is tucked into belted jeans. Dusty, black cowboy boots peek out under his rolled-up cuffs.

"Why not? It's just a pretend game anyway," I reply, as I inspect the perfectly good, short, flat stick that could have been a car. We had transformed the dirt into a fantasy world of large ranches, with stick-fences dividing his property from mine, and long country roads that meander through the play area alongside the dirt driveway. We're using those plastic cowboys that come in bags of hundreds as our rancher-selves.

"You just can't. That's the way it is," he says in his even, good-natured tone. "Here, use one of mine." He hands me an orange metal toy pick-up truck. I drop the stick and use the truck. At three years older, he's my tour guide in the ways of the world.

Our plastic toy selves seem real as we play in the flat area between the driveway and the creek bank, near Grandpa's five sheds that line the bank like a row of trees would do. I don't know what's in them, except for two. One houses a black, dusty 1930 Model A Coup which rests, lonely, unused, and with a history that I never thought to ask about. The other one is closest to our pretend ranches; Grandpa lets us use it as a playhouse. You would never know it used to be a poultry house, a home to chickens. It had been transformed. When you walk through the full-sized door, there's an old couch, a rug, and also a kitchen sink, refrigerator and stove built out of plywood and painted to look real by my dad, who has a talent for building things. In front of the playhouse is an ancient hand water pump that actually has water come out if you prime it. Of course, Grandma and Grandpa have running water, so it's never used except when Sandy, who has light brown hair and freckles and always wears dresses, pumps at it when we play house in the playhouse, so we can make mud pies and such. My dad always teases Sandy by calling her "Ignorance," so I grow up thinking that word is synonymous with her. Sandy responds to him by saying, "Ignorance is bliss." She's five years older than me, and doesn't always play with us anymore. She's getting to be a teenager.

I'm pushing my truck along one of our roads next to the creek bank when I lose my balance and tumble over the edge. I scream. I'm sliding fast, and see trees looming in my path. It's a long, steep trip to the bottom. Eddy turns, sees that I've disappeared over the bank, scrambles to the edge, falls to his stomach, reaches down and hollers, "Grab hold of me!" He manages to grab one of my wrists seconds before I'm out of reach and he yanks me to safety.

"Good thing you were there," I say, thinking how swift he is to get me before I'm gone, and how strong to pull me up. I'm feeling like he saved my life. I inspect for scrapes and brush the dirt off my clothes.

"Don't play so close to the edge," he warns, still in his calm manner.

"I don't even know how it happened," I answer.

"You were too close, that's all. Just stay over here." We return to our imaginary world, pushing trucks along dirt roads, visiting each other's ranches to borrow hay, or check on cattle. "Those are the things ranchers do," he tells me. "Someday I'll be a ranch manager. I won't ever have the money to own one, but I know I can be the manager." And I'm certain he can. Already, at eleven, he feeds Grandpa's calves with a nipple bucket and helps Grandpa cut and bale hay. He's been riding the tractor with Grandpa since he was a toddler, and he follows him around so much that his siblings call him "Daddy's Tail." None of the other kids took to farming the way Eddy did, and Grandpa took great pride in his little shadow. Eddy begged for a horse and finally Grandpa found an old swayback (probably getting it for free somewhere). Sometimes I get to ride Smokey, but usually only with Eddy in front, controlling the reins. Whenever Eddy dismounts, Smokey nips him in the heels as if to punish him for the ride. Sometimes Eddy ties a rope around the nose of a steer and rides it. Grandpa took a movie of him doing that once when Eddy got bucked off. He popped up from the ground with a huge grin on his face, eyes sparkling like he'd gone to heaven. In my eight-year-old mind, he's ready to be a ranch manager already. I love to follow him around to help do these things, but I don't want to be a rancher. I want to be a teacher, which I had decided one day in first grade at Teach School when my teacher, Mrs. Godfrey, was in a rocking chair reading a story to the class as we sat at her feet on the carpet.

Also in first grade in 1955, our class took a field trip to the Duveneck's farm next door to Grandma and Grandpa's. I wanted to run next door and show my class their farm too, but it didn't happen.

The Duvenecks had six kids and one of them, Chuck, was Eddy's friend. They ran back and forth between the two farms, playing cowboys and Indians, riding horses and riding on cows. There was a cow chute near the property line on the Duveneck side. They would get a cow into the chute, then one boy would get on the cow's back, while the other would let the gate open and out one would ride, like a bronco rider, laughing all the while. Every day they played "good cowboy and bad cowboy," with quick-draw contests to see who would be first to get the gun out of the holster. But Chuck was afraid of my Grandpa and would only come over when Grandpa wasn't home, which was after school until around five when Grandpa got home from work. Grandpa was stern with the boys. He didn't take much fooling around.

There was a day in first grade when Sandy, Eddy and I were all sick at the same time, so I stayed home from school at Grandma and Grandpa's house. We sure had fun upstairs, jumping up and down on Sandy's bed, while my unknowing Grandma was busy in the kitchen downstairs. I remember a few times staying there when I wasn't sick and I felt so happy to walk to school with Sandy and Eddy in the mornings.

Also in first grade, there was a line dividing the playground, an invisible barrier keeping the older kids away from first-graders. It might as well have been the Berlin Wall. You couldn't cross the line. I never dared to step across it, but at every recess I ventured to its edge to watch Eddy play foursquare for a few minutes while I boasted to my friends, "That's my uncle." He was a third grader and the foursquare game was adjacent to "the line." He was there every day, playing and laughing with his friends, adept with the ball, and looking well-groomed in his black, crew cut hair that Grandma always cut. His freckled face always had a quick, warm smile that made his green, friendly eyes sparkle. He always called himself "The Kid," and I think it's because it's what his grown brothers called him.

Even then I knew it was rare to have an uncle as a playmate. I had plenty of other uncles, grown ones. There were Eddy's older two brothers, my dad's three brothers, my maternal grandparents each had five siblings so there were many great-uncles plus the husbands of the aunts and great-aunts. My paternal grandparents had seven and thirteen siblings, meaning countless uncles on that side, so even at six, I understood it was unusual to go to school with your uncle. This uncle was like the big brother I never had. In my young mind, he *was* my big brother.

Chapter Four
Geneva Conference

Vietnam
1948–1956

The baby boy was growing up in a bamboo hut with an earthen floor, in a village of mostly peasants. It was a place where there were no cars and there might be only one bicycle in the village, owned by the wealthiest person. The boy was about nine, with dreams similar to his people, dreams of freedom. It was the time of the Vietnamese take-over of Dien Bien Phu, a fort-like base run by the French, in the northern part of Vietnam. The take-over was led by Ho Chi Minh, the Vietnamese Nationalist. After a three month battle, the French weakened. They surrendered the base on May 7th, 1954. The Vietnamese were happy and felt victorious. The news spread throughout the villages and trickled into the boy's tiny village. The adults talked of little else, and felt hopeful that Vietnam would be independent and would at long last rule itself. The boy and his people had suffered at the hands of the French for his entire life. He felt the pride of this victory along with his elders and he joined them in fiercely wanting his country to be independent. But unfortunately, peace for this little strip of a country was a long way off. There were other problems brewing. Stories found their way to the boy's village that the North Vietnamese communists were killing their own people. There were *horrible brutalities and there was fear in the air when the adults whispered about it.*

There are estimates that approximately 500,000 Vietnamese were killed by their own government during the 1950s. It was a time of terror. It was during this time of the French retreat and the communist genocide that a bigger war began, the war we call The Vietnam War but the Vietnamese call The American War. A conference between the United States, China, France and Vietnam, called the Geneva Conference, met to determine how to handle the situation. They made two agreements. The first was that there would be a ceasefire with the French and a division of the country along the 17th parallel. The communists, led by Ho Chi Minh, would control the north. The French would remain in the south. The second agreement was that neither side would form an alliance with any other country. But the United States refused to sign the second agreement, and instead moved in to South Vietnam to help protect it against communism. The theory was that if one country turned to communism other countries would follow, so the goal was to stop communist expansion. On November 1st, 1955, President Eisenhower sent a military advisory group to train the Army of the Republic of Vietnam (ARVN). This began the United States involvement in Vietnam.

After the split into north and south, the north allowed 300 days of free movement for northerners to move south if they chose to; approximately a million left the north. From these people who ventured south, the boy's family and neighbors heard stories of brutalities committed by the communists. In an unfair election, which was supported by the United States, Ngô Dinh Diêm proclaimed himself president of South Vietnam.

The boy didn't have anything to do with any of this, any of these political decisions, yet he was not even ten and he had lived through starvation, through revolution, through French domination, through fear of his own government, and he was now going to have to live through a bigger war, a war that seemed to have no end, but he didn't know that yet. What he did know was that, like the other villagers, he didn't like the French, and he didn't like the Americans moving in, and he wanted his country to be free to rule itself; even in his youth, he knew that.

Chapter Five
The Barn

California
1957–1960

My vision of years gone by was momentarily disturbed when a student drove into the parking lot, parked, and walked toward his apartment which was where the barn had been. I'm certain he could never imagine what I saw and what magical land was once right at this very place where he sleeps every night; nor did he even notice the sixty-year-old woman I had become who happened to be in the Stenner Glen parking lot doing what appeared to be nothing. Standing there, I saw and heard what wasn't there anymore—the barn, the chickens clucking, cows mooing, the many cats meowing, the dog barking, the breeze forever rustling through Eucalyptus trees. The student disappeared into his apartment as if he had been a commercial break in my fantasy, and then my personal movie screen rolled again.

"Come on," I say. "Let's go in the barn."

"You know we're not supposed to play in there," Eddy replies.

"Let's not play. Let's just go in and sit on the hay bales," I say. I love the barn more than any place on the farm. Actually, I suppose more than any place in the world.

He heads that way, and I follow, sort of skip-hopping because I'm so happy. "Ok," he says, "but no running, jumping, or climbing around. There's no telling what could happen. Then we'd be in for it!" Grandpa might get mad at him, but Grandpa would never get mad at me. He never did in all my life. There's something about being a granddaughter that feels like protection. My mom liked to tell that when she was pregnant with me, Grandpa would say, "Nobody's going to call me Grandpa," but the first moment he laid eyes on me, he cooed, "How's Grandpa's little girl?" My mom's diary from when she was little tells of a day she stayed home sick, and when Grandpa came home from work he brought her a rose. Grandpa had a soft side, despite the fact that he was stubborn and strict.

All of a sudden, my sister and brother are with us, clamoring to get into the barn too. Arthur shows up riding on Bouncer, their shiny-coated reddish cocker spaniel mix, as if on a horse. I think he and Judy were playing in the sandbox because Judy is covered with sand on her shorts. Any kind of dirt sticks to Arthur like a magnet so his hands are dark sand, like they'd been making mud pies. Judy has a blonde pixie haircut and when she smiles, you can see a big gap because her two front teeth are missing; they've been gone forever. Dad always sings her the Christmas carol, "All I want for Christmas is My Two Front Teeth." Eddy lifts the heavy wooden latch to the barn, and opens the giant, creaky door. Bouncer tries to go in, but Eddy says, "Bouncer! Stay!" Bouncer's ears nearly touch the ground when he hangs his head. We sneak in, all of us knowing we shouldn't be there.

There's nothing like it in the world. It's like entering a spacious castle, with high ceilings like a cathedral. Sunlight pours through the broken slats in the ceiling, spraying streaks of sunburst across the stacks and stacks of hay bales which fill the enormous barn. Some of the bales are missing, making stair steps. I climb up and sit high, feeling like I'm on a throne, and the smell is heaven. Chickens share my enthusiasm for the barn and I wonder why Grandpa lets them come in but not us. Arthur, who is six, feels the joy too and starts to tumble and roll around, so Eddy says, "We better get out of here." You can't always count on Arthur to behave. I have to lecture him sometimes and tell him that he wouldn't get into trouble so much if he just followed the rules. But overall, he's a nice boy. He's never mean. He just likes to tumble and play and doesn't always think about the rules.

"But Grandpa isn't even home," I complain. I'm not exactly considering the rules either because I know we're breaking a big one.

Eddy says, "Look what Arthur's doing. What if he ruins the bales? We'd be in hot water! Come on, let's go. Besides, Mom might catch us in here and tell Dad."

"Grandma wouldn't tell," I say.

"She might. And she'd be mad too. She knows we aren't supposed to be in here," he says.

But Grandma is probably so busy inside doing chores, I think she won't notice. That's where Sandy is too. Sandy helps her a lot unless she's sneaking away to read a Nancy Drew mystery upstairs in her quiet room. Mom told me she used to do the same thing—hide out with a book—but Grandma would always find her sooner or later and get her helping with the chores again. Grandpa comes home from work every day for lunch and sometimes Grandma fixes lunches so big they look like dinners. He works as foreman for the city water department. Sam the Listening Man is what a newspaper article wrote about him because he was always listening for water leaks. But after work, his real work begins. He runs the farm with four cows, and grows hay on the empty lot across the highway from the farm. One day he was running his tractor, cutting hay, when he suddenly turned off his engine without knowing why. Just then, one of my cousins, who was six, popped out of the tall hay directly in front of the tractor. Grandpa would have run over his grandson had he not cut the engine, and he marveled at the fact that some hidden force made him stop the tractor. My cousin lives across the street, the other direction from the farm, and had been playing there without Grandpa knowing.

I hate leaving the barn, that magical place, a palace, a cathedral with hay towers! We no sooner came out of the barn, and Eddy latches the gate, when Grandma pokes her graying head out the back screen door, and says, "Edward August, you didn't feed the cats and dog." We laugh at the close call that she didn't catch us in the barn.

Eddy hollers back in his musical, playful tone, "I'm halfway there already!" That's Eddy for you. He knows how to appease everyone.

On the west side of the barn there are six cow stalls, and sometimes I watch Grandpa milk the cows. He gives the cats the first squirt before he squirts the milk into the buckets. I like to go with Eddy to feed the calf, which is in a pen over by the avocado tree, closer to the creek bank. We put milk in the bucket that has a nipple, and then hold it for the calf to suck on. Near that calf pen is a place where the creek bank isn't so steep, and it makes climbing down easy, so we play in that area sometimes where there's lots of poison oak, and a trickle of water running through. It's a jungle of Eucalyptus and the ground is covered with its leaves, seed pods and strips of bark, all of which release the Eucalyptus aroma that fills my lungs and I fall in love with those trees in that creek bank. We sometimes climb the far bank to peek into the other world, the world of the Cal Poly campus, though we aren't allowed to cross the imaginary line at the top of the bank. But when I peek, it feels like a glimpse into a fairy tale world, like it jumped out of a story book.

Eddy has a bow and arrow that we shoot sometimes. He shows me how to load the arrow and pull back on it, and wham, I miss the target. He shows Judy and Arthur how to do it too, but Judy and I lose interest. Arthur likes it, and gets pretty good at it.

I was called back to the present again by a couple of students on bicycles, who crossed over the little bridge that leads them toward Cal Poly. I was standing in the parking lot in the same spot where the tank house was. The tank house stood majestically in the center of the circular, dirt driveway, defining the driveway, giving it its essence in much the way the Devil's Tower defines the flatlands between the Black Hills and the Big Horn Mountains. It was a tall, four-sided building that got narrower as it rose up toward a flat top which held a tank on top of it. At one time the tank held water that was forced into the pipes in the house so they would have running water, but that was long before my grandparents lived there. My grandmother used the building to store her canned peaches and pears. I think Grandpa kept the chicken feed in there too. There was a weathervane perched on top, like a star atop a Christmas tree.

Through the main entry—the back door—of the farmhouse was an enclosed porch lined by windows. That's where Grandma kept the mangle, a big steel-roll ironing machine that she used to iron sheets and clothes after they hung out to dry on a clothesline. The inside door from Grandma's porch led to an expansive, cheery kitchen where nourishing meals and plenty of desserts were made. Breakfast included freshly squeezed orange juice, straight from the trees out the back door, fresh eggs from the chickens, toast with Grandma's homemade boysenberry or plum jam, bacon or sausage, and chilled milk from the cows. Every morning Grandma filled two gallon-sized bottles with fresh milk after Grandpa had milked the cows, then she placed them in the refrigerator. Grandpa took the rest of the milk in metal cans down to the creamery. The world of my home and the world of Grandma's were very different. At home, the milkman delivered milk from a carton, right to our doorstep (probably from the creamery after Grandpa delivered his milk to them). At Grandma's, if you didn't drink the milk right away you would have to stir the cream back into the milk because it would separate and rise to the top.

Sometimes breakfast included Rice Krispies, and Grandpa had me believing that the little people—Snap, Crackle, and Pop—were actually in my cereal making the noises. At home, Mom didn't live in the kitchen like Grandma did. Orange juice was from a can. Breakfast was pretty much fix-your-own cereal except on weekends when we had French toast or pancakes. Lunch was a sandwich, and dinner was a nice, family meal, but with no dessert except ice cream later while watching TV. But Grandma, she must have spent most of her life in the kitchen for all the wonderful meals, pies, cakes and candies she prepared.

Grandma's kitchen had two exits (besides the one to the porch). One was straight ahead into a large dining room with hardwood floors. The other exited to the right of the room into a hallway that had stairs which led to the three upstairs bedrooms and the hall also led into a family room. At the base of the stairs was the phone, a party-line, which was mounted to the wall. The line was shared with other people, so sometimes if you picked it up to make a call, you heard voices. We were taught to hang up right away, that it was rude to listen. The family room and the dining room both led to the living room, completing the square, and you could loop in a circle through the whole downstairs. Throughout the house, there was an air of comfort, the way it feels to be wrapped in a warm blanket. The living room, though it still had the warm feel, through my childhood eyes, was a forbidden land. It was pristine and untouched but occasionally you could scoot through, making the complete circle of the downstairs rooms when chasing a sister, brother, cousin, Sandy or Eddy until

Grandma lost her patience and shooed us out to play with the chickens. In my home, we lived in our living room. But at Grandma's house we hung out in the family room, which had the TV, toys, comfy couch, chairs, and newspapers. We could play all we wanted in there, even while Grandpa was watching boxing on TV. Today, college apartments are located where the house once stood, but I could see it as vividly as if I were standing in that family room.

Eddy is lying on the couch watching TV. Judy whispers to me about how many freckles he has.

"Can we count your freckles?" Judy asks him. We are seven and eight and he is eleven.

"Why would you want to?" he asks.

"Because you have so many! They're all over your face, there must be a hundred. Can we count them?" I say, giggling.

"Ok," he replies. He shuts his eyes. He's calm, in patient silence as if in a deep meditation, while we start counting. He's always patient with his three nieces and seven nephews, and he lets everyone punch his stomach, hang on his arm, comb his hair or mess it up. He's like a serene mother duck, shepherding her line of ducklings. We soon realize counting his freckles is like counting grains of sand in the sandbox and we give up.

Later, Judy and I are coloring in a coloring book, when Judy asks him, "Whose do you like the best?"

He inspects both, then says, "Yours." But being as fair as he always is, he whispers to me, "I really like yours best, but didn't want to hurt her feelings." So now I'm happy too, and I believe him because I, of course, am older than Judy, and my coloring is clearly better because I can stay inside the lines. He shows us how to draw a surfer out of a question mark. I think it's clever, but not like Judy does. She takes it to heart, and draws it over and over, forever.

Every now and then Grandma has to wax her dining room floor. The first time I remember it, she called us kids in from outside to take off our shoes but leave the socks on.

"Come on!" Eddy says, "Do it like this!" In his socks, he speeds across the room, slipping and sliding from one end to the other, then zigzagging across the other way, hands flailing about, grinning from ear to ear. He has a contagious, wide smile that makes you feel happy.

"Wow, what fun! I can't believe Grandma is letting us do this," I say.

"It saves her polishing it," he replies, as he sails along. "Come on!" I'm tentative, but warm up to it. It's like roller skates or ice skates. Pretty soon we're all out there skating—Sandy, Eddy, me, Judy and Arthur. What fun to be skating on Grandma's floor in our socks.

There's a bird in the dining room, a blue parakeet named Blue Boy. He lives in a cage that stands atop a tall stand, next to the front window, but sometimes he's allowed to fly around the house. His favorite spot is the living room mirror where he perches on the top edge and peers down to see himself, then he talks to the bird in the mirror. Sometimes Eddy lets him sit on his head or shoulder. "Hey, look at this. I can walk with him sitting on my head and he won't fall off!" he says. "Wanna try?"

"No," I answer.

"Why not? He won't bite."

"I just don't want to. What if he poops or pees in my hair?"

He laughs. "He won't do that. He's never done that yet."

"There's always a first time."

"Shucks, let him sit on your finger then."

"No," I reply.

"Why not?"

"I don't know. He might bite, or scratch me. I don't like birds."

"How could you not like birds? Look at him. You're a hundred times bigger than him. He should be scared of you, not you of him. "

"I guess so," I say, as I reach out to pet him, trying to be brave.

Sometimes we have ice cream at Grandma's, and Eddy taught me to stir the chocolate sauce and the vanilla ice cream until it is a silky, smooth, chocolatey, yummy dessert that we slurp from our spoons. As we finish our final slurps, he says, "I know a way to get every last drop."

"Lick the bowl?" I ask.

"Better."

"How then?"

"Follow me." I trail him to the kitchen from the family room. He goes to the sink, turns on the faucet and places his bowl under the water until he has enough to cover the bottom. He swishes the water around until he gets the ice cream off the sides, as you would do when rinsing the bowl, getting ready to do the dishes.

I think he's cleaning it, so I ask, "So, ok, how do you get more?" Then, right before my eyes, he drinks the bowl of dirty water.

He looks at me with proud eyes, as if he'd won a trophy. "It's good," he says, justifying himself. "Go on, try it. It's good. And it's the last drop, like I said."

"But it's dishwater! It's filthy."

"Try it, it's just ice cream mixed with water. It gets the last bit, and it's worth it."

I try it. "It *is* good. It's like ice cream flavored water."

"Told you!" He still looks as proud as if he had discovered electricity or something.

One sunny afternoon, like most of them were, Eddy is wearing a black cowboy hat trimmed in white, play guns in a holster, and chaps as we play cowboys and Indians. He has spare guns that Judy and I use. Arthur brought his own. I wore my own red cowboy hat. All of us run around the circular driveway, chasing and shooting at each other, sometimes hiding from each other behind a shed.

I gallop on my imaginary horse behind Eddy on the driveway along the length of the lawn when I shoot him. "Gotcha," I holler.

He stops in his tracks, his hat slips to the side, and he turns to tell me, "If you get shot, count to ten, then you come back to life."

"But you can't *really* come back to life if you're killed," I say, having already learned about death when both of our cats, Inky and Pierre, died suddenly of a viral disease.

"But we're playing. Just count to ten, then you can be alive again. It's ok, we can make the rules how we want them."

"Ok," I say, realizing it wouldn't be fun to be out of the game.

So Eddy freezes, counts out loud to ten, then gallops off, as if on a racing horse, waving his gun in the air, with his hat flopping around. I follow behind, waving my gun too, just like him.

We go to the movies on Saturday afternoons in the summer. My dad is PTA president, and he started a fundraiser for the school. It's a coupon book for Saturday afternoon movie marathons at the Fremont Theatre downtown. The money made from selling the coupon books is split between the school and the theatre. The coupon book is good for every Saturday throughout the summer. Everybody in town drops their kids off at the theatre and we watch movies all afternoon. It's always a full house, packed with kids, no adults. There are contests and ticket-stub drawings for prizes during breaks between movies. It's a wild place. The movies are always westerns. Every single movie, Eddy leans over and says, "Which guy are you?"

"The Indian," I say every time. "How about you?"

"The cowboy," he answers. He's forever being the good cowboy. The one who saves the day. And every movie, I'm the good Indian. I love being the Indian.

One Saturday, Sandy and Eddy sit directly behind me. Judy is on one side of me; a boy who came with us is on the other. The boy is younger, but he's bigger than me. He's almost as tall as Eddy. At one point he leans over and tries to kiss me. I turn around and complain to Sandy and Eddy. The next thing I know Eddy comes around to my row, stands directly in front of him and says, "Get up."

"Why?" he asks.

"Get up. You're sitting in the back with Sandy." He doesn't even think to argue because Eddy means business. Eddy takes his seat as the boy slinks away toward the row behind, and again, I think of Eddy as my hero. He is, in fact, the good cowboy.

There's a water reservoir in the back yard of the farm that holds water that eventually becomes the cows' drinking water. It's about ten by ten feet, five feet high, made of cement with a small deck along one side and stairs leading to the top of it, built by Grandpa. The deck is only about two feet wide, but it's big enough to stand on in order to get into the reservoir which acts as our swimming pool. In the summer months we splash and swim, and the parents lounge on folding chairs on the lawn; blankets and towels are strewn across the grass. We eat oranges straight from trees that shade us when it gets too hot. Usually my four cousins, John, Mike, Mark and Sammy and their mom and dad, Carl and Emily, are there, and our family, and Grandma, Grandpa, Sandy and Eddy.

My other cousins, Linda, Danny, and Richard, moved to San Diego but sometimes they're with us too. Sometimes Chuck, the neighbor boy, joins us. One day, I fall off my raft and sink under water. Somehow my dad is suddenly there pulling me out from the deep. He gets me out of the tank and when I catch my breath and regain composure, I want to go back in. Dad says, "You want in again? I thought you'd be done after that experience." I think he was a little impressed.

"Nope. I'm going in," I say. I want to be able to swim like Sandy and Eddy. They swim like fish back and forth, across the little pool and even under-water swimming, which I don't like to do. When they were little, Grandpa kept only two feet of water in it, until they learned to dog-paddle. As they got bigger, he increased the water level to three feet, and as they improved in their swimming skills he filled it higher. Eddy likes to stand backwards on the edge of the pool and dive backwards. We have a movie of him doing that over and over again at my great aunt's swimming pool in Santa Rosa. Every time he pops up from the water after the dive he has a huge grin, and he climbs out to do it again.

Grandpa made a go-cart for Eddy and we often get to take turns riding while Eddy drives, putting around the tank house and on a narrow path behind the sheds along the edge of the creek, which is scary for me since I almost fell down it once. But on this day, Eddy, who is thirteen, gets it out and it won't start. He pulls on the rope, but it's like a stubborn lawn mower. The engine won't turn over no matter what. "I'm going to get Chuck to see if he can start it," he says. He takes off running for the neighboring farm.

Arthur is eight years old, and without a word he takes the cord and pulls on it like he saw Eddy do. The engine revs up.

"But I don't know how to drive it," he says. Judy and I didn't know how either.

We wait a minute for Eddy to return and he doesn't. Arthur shuts it off. We're convinced it'll start again when he returns.

Finally, he shows up with Chuck. Arthur says, "It works now."

"What do you mean?" Eddy has a puzzled expression.

"I pulled the cord and it started, but I turned it off."

"What? You turned it off? Why?" Eddy says, perplexed.

"I didn't want you to get mad, and we don't know how to drive it," Arthur explains, sheepishly. I don't know why he would think Eddy would get mad since I had never seen him mad before.

Eddy and Chuck take turns pulling the cord. It doesn't start. They keep trying for a while but nothing happens.

Eddy stands up, exasperated with the thing. "Arthur, you should have left it running. Looks like we won't be riding the go-cart today."

Eddy went to Chuck's to play and we had to go home anyway. We find out later that Chuck has a bunch of horses they got for the summer from his relatives. Some are wild. Chuck dared Eddy to get on one and ride it. Eddy loves to ride, so he gets on one with no reins, no saddle. Chuck whacks the horse on the rear. The horse takes off like a wild bronco. Eddy holds its mane and rides it like a bronco rider. He stays on, but later he says what a wild ride it was. When he gets off, he laughs along with Chuck who is in hysterics. He doesn't hold a grudge against Chuck for knowing the horse would do that.

I felt the pull, like the pull of a tide, to remain in the past in the happy days of childhood on the farm. I didn't want to leave but I had stood long enough in the student housing parking lot. Somberly, I climbed into my car, started the engine and headed out the driveway, yet I felt like I was driving away from my past. As I drove out of the parking lot, I couldn't help but recall the long dusty driveway of Grandma and Grandpa's farm and walking it when I would spend the night and walk to school with Sandy and Eddy. I turned left at the end of the driveway, south on Highway 1, toward San Luis Obispo. On my left at the first corner was the Zion Lutheran Church. When it was newly built, and Sandy and Eddy were seven and five they started going there for Sunday school. The Duvenecks remember seeing them walk along the highway, past their property every Sunday morning. Eddy was in dress slacks, white shirt and bow tie. Sandy was in a pretty Sunday dress, with a little hat atop her brown wavy hair. Eddy took to Sunday school with the devotion of a duck to water, and was baptized at the same time as Sandy, in June of 1958, when he was eleven. After two years of classes, at age thirteen, he went through confirmation, which was held on June 5th, 1960. Pastor Stan Quebe performed the ceremony and gave him a little book titled *Living for Christ.* In it he wrote, "Dear Edward, May you always live for HIM who died for you! God's richest blessings! Pastor Quebe & family." Eddy followed the advice in that little book and kept it with his special things.

In that Sunday school class was a little girl named Maryanne who also had ranching in her blood, and Eddy noticed her even then, although she was in the class behind him. Grandma and Grandpa began going to that church every Sunday, which they had not done before, and they continued to do so until the end of their lives. We have a home movie of Eddy's confirmation day. He's dressed in a white gown over his dress clothes, holding his certificate. Sandy is teasing him. She repeatedly taps him on the back as he playfully bats her away each time. Both of them are smiling wide, happy smiles.

Erma, Grandpa, Mom, Carl; 1939.

Gary, Sandy, Eddy, Grandpa; 1947.

Sandy, me, Eddy; 1950.

Grandma, Grandpa, Sandy, Eddy.

Sandy, Eddy, me; 1952.

Judy, Mom, Arthur, Dad, and me; circa 1952.

Eddy on Smokey; circa 1956.

Some of Eddy's nieces and nephews;
Thanksgiving 1955.

Eddy in his usual home attire; circa 1957.

Playing "quick draw" with his friends; circa 1957.

The front of the farm house.

Eddy in front of the barn and tank house, with cats and
Bouncer, the dog.

Christmas 1957.   Eddy with Blue Boy, the parakeet.

Judy and me on Smokey.

Eddy on the go-cart that
Grandpa built.

Eddy riding a steer, with the
farm in background.

Eddy's confirmation; June 1960.

Chapter Six
Viet Cong

Vietnam
1959–1962

The boy had never known freedom from fear, but extreme terror grew in his land when he was an early teen. After 1959, North Vietnam sent 20,000 Viet Cong (cong means communist) troops south to conquer South Vietnam. Within a year, approximately 1,500 South Vietnamese civilians were killed and about 700 more were missing. The people of his village lived in constant fear. The villagers heard stories that civilians, including women and children, were being tortured. In 1961, approximately a hundred southern villages were destroyed monthly, so President Kennedy sent 400 military men to train the South Vietnamese to defend themselves. But the number of Viet Cong increased; they included both guerilla and regular army units and were referred to as the NLF (National Liberation Front). By 1962 they were destroying not a hundred, but approximately a thousand villages every month. In addition to the brutalities and attacks by the North Vietnamese, South Vietnam was ruled by Diêm, who was a corrupt leader. Diêm didn't allow Buddhist activities, despite that Buddhism was the main religion. The boy was like others in his village: they hated Diêm, hated the French, hated the Americans. They wanted them all out of their country. He could taste freedom and independence. His desire was strong. The communists, like the boy, *wanted the north and south to be one. He had known fear and oppression his entire life. Like many of his peers, rather than be destroyed and mutilated by the Viet Cong, in order to fight for a unified Vietnam, he joined with the communists as a Viet Cong soldier.*

Chapter Seven
Future Farmer

California
1961–1963

Grandma and Grandpa moved from the farm they had leased for sixteen years, the Steiner place they called it. The owners wanted to sell, so there wasn't much they could do. The new owners wanted to rent it to them month by month but Grandpa said you can't farm a month at a time, so they moved. My mother had lived on that farm as an older teenager, and I got to play there as a child, but now it became only a memory. It was in December of 1960, nine months before I started seventh grade. At eleven, though my playing years were about over anyway, I felt the loss. Yet like the pearl within an oyster, the joy of those days lives within, defining me.

Grandma and Grandpa bought a house in a residential neighborhood on Cecilia Court. Eddy was fourteen and Sandy was sixteen when they moved. After living their whole lives there, the farm not only defined them but it *became* them as simply as a sunflower seed becomes a sunflower or an acorn becomes an oak. Eddy didn't just want to become a rancher—he *was* one, it was in his heart and blood, but now he had no farm or ranch. It's who he was though. Sandy continued to do the things Grandma taught her to do on the farm: cooking, growing things, canning, sewing. Throughout her life she became very much an earth mother, living simply, caring for her six children and many grandchildren with more still to come. Since Grandma and Grandpa hadn't moved to the farm until their older kids were teenagers, the older three didn't have farming in their blood the way Sandy and Eddy did. My mother was the furthest thing from an "earth mother" and, for her, well, she was a modern 1950s housewife and appreciated the new conveniences, like vegetables in a can and milk delivered at the door. Once her kids were older, she returned to work and became personal secretary to the county engineer. Gary, her brother, became an engineer for Cal Trans and Carl, her other brother, became a truck driver. Farming was in none of them. We'll never know what Erma would have done.

Maybe it's because Eddy was Grandpa's "little shadow" that Grandpa took an interest in everything Eddy did. Grandpa never went to Gary's baseball games in high school, but anything Eddy did, he went to it. Mom remembers walking from the farm all the way to town because Grandpa wouldn't drive her to places she wanted to go, yet Eddy got a car when he was sixteen. Maybe it was because Grandpa realized he had done it wrong the first time with the older kids. Maybe he wanted to do it right with this last-chance baby. Whatever the reason, Eddy was favored and it didn't go unnoticed by the others. But then, Eddy was favored by everyone. There was just something about him.

On my twelfth birthday in October 1961 my parents gave me a transistor radio, which was a small pocket-sized radio popular with teens. Grandma, Grandpa, Sandy and Eddy came for my birthday dinner. I turned my radio to the station my parents listened to which played their kind of music from the forties, like the Big Bands, Frank Sinatra and Dean Martin.

"What are you listening to?" Eddy asks. He's in a plaid, button-up, short-sleeved shirt, tucked into jeans, with a white T-shirt peeking above the top button on his shirt.

"KVEC," I say.

"Let me see that thing," he says. He fiddles with the dial and hands it back to me. "This is what you should be listening to: KSLY. It plays the cool songs."

"Okay," I say. I take it and plug my earplugs back in. Alvin, Simon and Theodore, the chipmunks, are singing and I realize Eddy knows the cool stuff to do so I stay on KSLY after that.

Eddy was in ninth grade that year, so we were in the same school again at the junior high. It was natural for him to join Future Farmers of America (FFA), being the aggie that he was in his heart. It's no wonder I hardly saw him at school because in one year he made a gate latch, a show stick, a wood float, and a nail box. He also added a handle to a hammer and sharpened a screwdriver, all for the purpose of showing at three different local fairs—King City, Santa Maria, and the Mid-State Fair in Paso Robles. He must have been in the woodshop and agriculture rooms during every break in order to get all of that made in time for the fairs. He ended up with first or second place ribbons on all.

Not only did Grandma and Grandpa move that year, but my family moved too, out of the home we'd been in since I was four. Some days from the past blend with others in a blur, as if fast-forwarding through a DVD. But when you stop the fast forward and watch a scene, that's how it is with monumental life moments. I might as well be there now the memory is so vivid, because the slice of time was life-altering.

Awhile after I turned twelve, my family is at the dinner table. Dad surprises us by asking, "Would you kids rather have a horse or a new baby?"

"A horse!!!!" the three of us shout simultaneously. Could it be true? Was this one of his jokes? He always plays jokes on us, like short-sheeting the bed, or hiding a piece of cloth inside our pancakes so when you bite into it there is something there. Judy was too little at the time to get the humor of that so she cried and wailed over it like the cloth had attacked her or something. I wonder where we'll keep the horse now that Grandma's farm is gone. I'm more excited than if he'd said we were heading to Disneyland. I'd always, desperately, wanted a horse. When I was ten, a friend and I secretly sent away for greeting cards to sell after seeing an ad in a magazine. We hoped to make enough money to buy a horse. When the greeting cards arrived, Mom was upset with me and made me send them back. She was very protective and didn't want me going door to door to strangers' homes.

Dad seems surprised by our reaction and quickly adds, "Sorry, it's not a horse. We're going to have a baby."

"A baby? A baby?" We are stunned. We are ten, eleven, and twelve. It had been the three of us forever and I always thought that was a fixed thing, unchangeable, like the way the sun rises and sets every day, like the way the North Star shines every night in the north. I have no idea of how babies are made, and for some reason with this new event I don't even speculate on it. It's simply a new fact that I take in, just as I know that though the sun always shines, sometimes there's an eclipse. We're so excited that we jump out of our chairs and run up and down the hall. We're screaming and jumping and we're the happiest, noisiest children in the world to think that we're going to have a new baby. I think Mom and Dad feel satisfied to see our eagerness because when we thought we were getting a horse we felt excited but we didn't scream, run or jump. This is better, way better, and they feel happy with our reaction.

The pre-baby months drag on. I'm impatient, but we're occupied because we have to move. Mom and Dad say our house is too small so we sell it and find a house to lease in Atascadero, a smaller town a few miles north. I help Dad with the packing because Mom needs bed rest the last half of the pregnancy. Our new house is a beautiful Spanish style, with five bedrooms, three bathrooms, a dining room, a breakfast room, a kitchen and a walk-in pantry. A playroom is under the house. You have to go outside to get to the entrance of it, which for some reason, feels exotic to me that we kids have our own private entrance to our own playroom.

Karen enters our world on July 29th, 1962. Dad comes home from the hospital and the three of us clamor for details.

"What does she look like?" I ask.

"Like Edward G. Robinson," he responds, chuckling.

"Who's that?" I ask, turning up my nose, thinking this doesn't sound good. I expected to hear how beautiful she is.

"An actor with a scrunched face and lots of dark hair," he says, then laughs that deep-hearted laughter of his.

"Really, Daddy? She's not cute?" I wonder, and feel worried.

"She looks just like you guys did. She'll turn out alright," he says. He adds, "Remember that Judy looked like a bug when she came along and that's why we call her Bugs, but she turned out pretty darned cute, didn't she? Karen will be the same."

A couple of days later they bring her home. Grandma, Grandpa, Sandy and Eddy can't wait to see her and drive over Cuesta Grade to be here for her homecoming. My dad is right about some of it. She has tons of black hair, but her face doesn't look so scrunched up. She looks like the most beautiful baby I've ever seen. But we are frustrated with her because she sleeps so much. Eddy, Judy, Arthur and I play on the Slip 'n Slide outside her window and we shout, scream and laugh louder than normal because we want to wake her up. But she sleeps on and on. Finally when she wakes up, we each get a chance to hold her. She has so many caretakers that we argue over who gets to hold her, feed her, and change her.

On Christmas 1962, Grandma, Grandpa, Sandy and Eddy came for dinner. A home movie shows Karen, at six months, sitting on a blanket on the living room floor. Her hair has lightened from black to a light brown, almost blonde. Eddy, at sixteen, is lying on the floor, on his side, elbow propped to hold his head in his hand. He's looking at Karen, talking to her, telling her to look at the camera and to wave. He looks at the camera and flashes that wide smile that makes everyone around fill with sun-like energy. Eddy has matured into a young man of short height but strong shoulders and muscles due to baling hay during the summers.

Now that Eddy could drive, Grandpa took him to buy his first car from an English lady who invited them in for tea and vanilla ice cream. Sandy, who went with them, politely said no thank you to the ice cream because she didn't like vanilla, and she knew Eddy didn't either, but she suddenly heard Eddy ask, "Do you have any chocolate syrup?" The English lady did not. But he did leave with his first car, a dark green Austin, which had been sitting in her garage for a few years because her husband had died and she didn't drive. Instead of turn indicator lights, the car had turn indicators that popped up like little arms announcing which direction he was going to turn. They were attached to the frames between the front door and the back door and he controlled them with the flick of a switch. We giggled about how it looked like a puppet. Some of his friends made fun of it calling it names like "Green Peanut," and someone wrote in his yearbook: "hot boy with a little foreign car."

Eddy never missed church on Sunday, even though they no longer lived next door to it. He drove across town to get there, but it was more important to him than anything else. He was very close to God, yet it was private with him. There was only one time he talked to me about it. He wondered why I didn't go anymore. I told him what had happened with the Sunday school teacher in Atascadero who had called me at home to tell me I would go to Hell if I chose to go to the school party instead of the Sunday school party, making me cry. After that, my dad told my mom that he didn't want us going to Sunday school anymore, and he went down to that church and had a word with that woman. Eddy didn't try to convince me to go to church, but he quietly told me how important it was to him.

Maryanne had been in Sunday school with him for years, but in the class below him, so he hadn't gotten to know her. Now they were both in Walther League, the Lutheran group for teens. Whenever she was in the room, he sneaked glances when she wasn't looking, but felt tongue-tied at the thought of talking with her. In everything else in life he was efficient, capable and strong, but in this, whenever he would see her, he was unsure.

One thing about Eddy is that he was the hardest worker I ever knew. He was perfect for FFA because he was responsible, dedicated and smart. During his sophomore year, he made a rope halter, a spade, a picnic bench, a stanchion, and entered them in King City, Santa Maria and Paso fairs and earned either first or second place on all. He wanted to take an animal to the Mid-State Fair in Paso, so Grandpa found him a good quality market lamb, and also a ram and some ewes so he could breed them. They found a farm on Orcutt Road where they could lease land for his herd.

It was the summer of 1963 when Sandy, at eighteen, left home to work in Yosemite. She had graduated from high school the year before. At thirteen, I felt shocked that she moved out. It was the first time I'd considered that kids do grow up and move away.

Mid-day at the Paso fair you could feel as hot as if you'd stuck your head in an oven. And the bunkhouse, where Eddy stayed, felt exactly like one. They kept a fan going but all it did was push around the hot air. At night they kept the door open to let the cooler air in but it was still hot. They slept in sleeping bags on cots but most often the heat forced them to sleep on top of their bags. His FFA teacher, Mr. Williams, was a stickler about getting them up before dawn to clean the stalls, sweep the cement aisle in front of the stalls and feed and water their animals. He wanted his club to win the clean stall award, but mostly he wanted the boys to learn responsibility and to take pride in a job well done. He didn't have trouble getting Eddy to do any of it. Responsibility was his middle name.

It was August 1963. Eddy loved early morning sights and sounds of the animal barns when the air was cooler, warm but not yet hot, and the only people were 4-H and FFA kids because it was hours before the fair would open at 10 a.m. But it was the smell he loved the most, the smell of straw on the cement floors of the open-air barns and the medley of odors from pigs, lambs, steers, heifers, and horses. The squealing pigs, baaing sheep, mooing cows, and the sound of busy kids bathing their pigs, cleaning their stalls, sheering their sheep and sweeping their aisles clean, were all things he relished. He took to this life like a bird takes to the air. He was not afraid of hard work, in fact, he thrived on it. And every now and then he got a glimpse of Maryanne, who was judging animals for 4-H, and one day, when he felt brave, he walked over to ask her something about Walther League. When she smiled, he hoped he would eventually get the nerve to ask her for a date.

On the day of the showmanship contest, the boys in his bunk house were nervous, even those who had done it before, and especially the first-timers like Eddy. But his lamb was ready and so was he. He had spent many hours practicing. Part of showmanship is looking good yourself. He made sure his boots were shined, his white pants spotless, his dark blue, corduroy FFA jacket unwrinkled. When he was in the holding pen, prior to his turn in the ring, he probably took a deep breath and said a prayer. Out in the ring, he remained focused and concentrated on keeping his eyes on the judge. He knew that when the judge looked at him he had better be looking at the judge. When the judge turned from him he could inspect his lamb and adjust what he needed to. But he had to keep glancing at the judge to make sure he didn't miss when the judge looked his way. When it was over, they called names to reenter the ring, to receive ribbons. He held his breath, hoping to hear his name. There it was: Edward Schultz. He took his lamb into the ring, and gladly received the fifth place ribbon. With only ten entrants to get a ribbon, out of at least fifty kids showing their lambs, he felt he had done well for his first time. Two days later was market day. Again, he dressed carefully for the event, took his lamb into the ring, along with many other kids and their lambs, and ended up getting a first place ribbon in his division, and at the end, he received reserve grand champion, meaning Grandpa had done well picking out a lamb that was well built, and Eddy had done well in feeding it properly so that it would grow into a worthy market lamb.

At the time the fair was going on, my parents bought a house in San Luis Obispo on Augusta Street, three blocks from Grandma and Grandpa's new place. So after living in Atascadero for a year, we were close to my grandparents again, but on the opposite side of town from where we had all been before. And both families, ours and theirs, were about two miles from where Eddy's sheep were kept on Orcutt Road.

After Eddy's breakthrough conversation with Maryanne at the fair, he felt a surge of confidence to talk with her again at the Walther League meetings. He liked her friendly eyes, soft curls and confident manner. She had fair, clear skin, with light brown hair, and her sweet, fresh look appealed to him. They both became leaders of the group which meant travelling to Santa Maria or Arroyo Grande to join with other youth group leaders, then to report back to the local group. Walther League also sponsored beach parties and snow trips, and these activities helped Eddy to feel more comfortable around her. They laughed easily together and thought the same things were funny. He wondered if she would go on a date with him, but he was afraid to ask. There were other boys who liked her too.

Chapter Eight
Diêm

Vietnam
1962–1963

Diêm was a harsh, oppressive and corrupt leader. His regime in South Vietnam acted brutally toward Buddhists by attacking their pagodas, tearing down their flags, arresting them and sometimes killing them. Some Buddhist monks protested by burning themselves to death. The people were angry and the boy felt as they all did. They hated Diêm and felt he was an extension of the French who had oppressed them. They were also angry at the Americans for sending support. All they wanted was peace in their land, and unification of the northern and southern parts of their country. The boy knew he'd made the right decision to become a Viet Cong soldier. He was swift, light on his feet, slipped in and out of the underground tunnel network with ease, and had honed his skills in his three years of soldiering by the time he turned seventeen.

The boy wanted Diêm out, and wanted the Americans out. But the opposite was happening. More Americans were coming in. In August of 1962 President Kennedy signed an act allowing for military support to any country being attacked by communists. In November of 1963, not long before he was assassinated, President Kennedy increased the military personnel in Vietnam to 16,000. They were sent to train South Vietnamese soldiers *to fight the communists.*

Kennedy didn't agree with Diêm's ways, but he was not against Diêm like the people of South Vietnam were. He was more concerned with the communism of North Vietnam. But the South Vietnamese hated Diêm and rose up against him in a coup and killed him. The people cheered and the Buddhists were relieved. The boy felt as everyone else did, that there might be hope for unification of north and south.

Chapter Nine
Graduation

California
1963–1966

When school started in the fall of 1963, Eddy was a junior and Maryanne, a sophomore. I was in ninth grade at the junior high. The high school was down the hill from the junior high, had been newly built, and had many windows in the central area where the office and lockers were, so it was always light and had an open feel, almost like being outside. Within the first days, Eddy saw Maryanne near his locker and luckily discovered that hers wasn't far from his. There was something about seeing her that made everything else blur into the background. After a couple of weeks, he managed to get up his courage to ask her to a movie. She accepted and they had such a good time that he invited her to a football game, and again, when her eyes sparkled, and her smile flashed, he knew he wanted to keep seeing her. They laughed a lot together. October 11th, 1963 was the Backwards Dance, and Maryanne invited Eddy. They were off to a great start with each other.

Around that time, Eddy bought a fixer-upper '58 Ford Ranchero, which, although it was a pick-up, I thought its body looked like a station wagon without the top half. After restoring the engine, he took it to the city yard where Grandpa worked and he painted it copper. I wondered how he knew how to restore an engine, and paint a car, but he did it and it looked good. Once it was restored, he kept it as spotless as freshly cleaned windows. He sold the Austin, which had served him well, but like an artist who needed paints, he was a farmer who needed a truck.

Eddy was elected vice-president of FFA and consequently became friends with Tom St. John, who was president. Tom was a senior, and claims he's the worst thing that ever happened to Eddy. Tom was one of those people who had a quick and easy smile that whispered mischief. His eyes twinkled with the delight of his escapades. Tom encouraged Eddy to have a few beers, play a few pranks and let loose a little bit. But he says to this day that he never met anyone nicer than Eddy.

In November of 1963, just before President Kennedy was assassinated, Eddy and his lamb made the *Telegram Tribune.* A few months later a picture of him was in the paper again, this time on a tractor. The article tells how FFA students leased acreage where they could grow hay. Eddy grew his on fifteen acres on Laurel Lane.

I didn't know anyone who worked as hard as Eddy, or got as much done, and he always had a smile and good humor. He was the most easy-going person I ever knew. I can't remember ever seeing him riled, rushed or upset about anything. He made hard work look like a breeze. During this school year he made a calf pen which earned first place at the King City fair. He also made a picnic table which earned first at the Santa Maria fair. He not only raised a lamb for the Paso fair, but he also decided to take a steer. Grandpa knew enough about steers to locate a good one for him. They leased land on Terrace Hill, which was near their house, so Eddy could keep his steer there.

He drove his Ranchero up and down Augusta Street every morning before school and again after school to feed his steer on the hill at one end of Augusta, and then to feed his sheep and horse beyond the other end of Augusta on Orcutt Road. He passed our house on his way to the sheep, so he stopped every day to see who wanted to go with him. I went a few times, but I was involved in the school drama department, usually staying after school to rehearse for plays, and on weekends and summers I was usually at the beach. Judy went with him sometimes and remembers feeding his lambs Nestle candy bars to fatten them up when they might not make weight for the fair. Arthur went often, and he ended up following in Eddy's footsteps by also raising lambs for the fair. But Karen, starting when she was about three, was the one who went the most because she didn't have the social life the rest of us had. She loved to stand on the fence and watch him feed his sheep and his horse, Cayenne (his first horse, Smokey, had eventually died). After the feeding, Eddy would stop to drop Karen off, and he would linger around until it was time for dinner. He would smell what was cooking, and finally ask what was cooking. I think he decided whether to eat with us or at Grandma's based on what was cooking at each place. I loved when he stayed for dinner.

That August, moving his gear into the bunkhouse at the fair for the second time felt like coming home. He was more experienced this time and knew the other guys better. They were all hard workers, but they liked to goof off and have fun too, like spraying each other with hoses when temperatures climbed over a hundred. He liked this year better for another reason. He didn't have to make up excuses to go to the 4-H barn to "accidentally" run into Maryanne. This time she was his girlfriend, and they could walk around the fair together. Their club didn't allow them to be out late and mostly they were busy taking care of their animals or in their competitions, but a couple of times, he and Maryanne were able to walk the fair, holding hands, looking at exhibits and going on carnival rides. They had lots of fun together, and conversation flowed. He showed animals on four of the days during fair week—both his lamb and steer in both market and showmanship. Both animals received a first place ribbon in market class and he placed in the top ten for showmanship. Saturday was the auction and both animals sold. He received his check on Sunday, the day they packed for home. That morning in August of 1964, he watered his animals for the final time and said good-bye, knowing they were going to slaughter, but feeling okay with that because that's why they had been bred.

He deposited his check at the bank on Monday morning and began his search for a car to take Maryanne on dates. He found a black and white '56 Pontiac. He didn't sell his Ranchero, so now he had two cars. To support the cars and dating, in addition to baling hay, he got a job at Madonna Inn, waiting tables in the café.

At this time, in 1964, approximately half of Americans had never heard of Vietnam. I hadn't, and I doubt if Eddy had.

During his senior year in 1964-65, Eddy was elected FFA president and earned the State Farmer award. Oddly, nobody from San Luis High earned the State Farmer award again until my brother, Arthur, earned the same award and was also FFA president a few years later in 1972. There must be a genetic component because many years later my daughter, Lindsey, was FFA president at Atascadero High, and earned the same award, the State Farmer award in 1998, thirty-three years after her great-uncle and twenty-six years after her uncle.

Uncle Carl moved his family to San Jose, a three hour drive away. My cousin, John, the oldest of four boys, says the reason he joined FFA at San Jose High School was because of Eddy. He claimed he not only wanted to be like Eddy, he wanted to *be* Eddy. But that would be impossible for John, for though he had a good heart, and as much as he wanted to be like Eddy, he often got into his share of mischief (and cheated at Monopoly). Unlike Eddy, who always knew the right thing to do, even as a child; it was almost like Eddy was born grown-up. But I've known a lot of grown-ups who weren't as mature as Eddy, so I suppose another way to put it is that he was good to the core.

I started at the high school as a sophomore that year. He said it was weird to see me "running around" at the high school and that's what he wrote in my yearbook at the end of the year. At first, I teased him by calling him "Uncle Eddy" at school but he didn't like it and told me so.

I think it embarrassed him, so I quit doing it and went back to calling him "Eddy" like I'd always done. He was the type of guy in school who was quiet, polite, and handsome with dark hair, stocky shoulders, and beautiful smile. Lots of girls had crushes on him despite his shyness. "Ed Schultz is your uncle?" girls would say to me and Judy. They wanted us to fix them up with him. But that was out of the question because he had fallen for Maryanne. There was one girl who not only had a crush on him, but kept pestering him with phone calls. She told me later how obnoxious she'd been, chasing after him, but that he had always been polite. I hadn't met Maryanne yet but I'd been hearing about her. I knew they had church and the fair in common and they'd been dating awhile. The day I met her seems like yesterday.

"Are you going to the dance Friday night?" he asks, during my second week at the high school.

"Yes," I reply, "why?"

"I want you to meet Mim," he responds, rather shyly. Mim was his nickname for Maryanne.

I'm at the dance on Friday and can't find them. It's a crowded, packed room, and dark. Finally I find them. As I meet Maryanne, and talk with her, I think if I could have picked anyone for him, I would have chosen her. She's just right for a guy as nice as Eddy. She's pretty in a sweet way. Nice, friendly eyes. She has a quiet demeanor yet is quick to smile. She's slender with semi-curly and soft, short light brown hair. I'm proud of him for his choice.

After meeting Maryanne, I look for my friends and I'm oblivious of a cleared area on the dance floor so I walk right through it. It had been cleared of people because there was broken glass on the floor. Unknowingly, I walk over the glass and because I'd taken off my shoes for the dancing, I cut my foot and it's bleeding profusely. A classmate helps me stop the bleeding, but I go home as it's a deep cut. The next time I see Eddy he says, "Where were you? I came back to the dance after taking Maryanne home and I looked everywhere for you. I wanted to ask you for a dance," he says.

It would have been my first and only time to ever have a dance with Eddy. We were never at another dance at the same time again.

I always thought it a coincidence that it was Maryanne's family ranch, twenty-two years before, where Mom and Dad had their first date on a hayride, a blind date. Maryanne had a little brother who was the same age as Karen so she and Eddy always compared notes about the little ones. She would say that her brother was doing this or that, and Eddy would say that Karen was doing this or that, always trying to top each other.

One Saturday, Eddy had to haul sixty bales of hay across town to where he kept his sheep. He asked Arthur to help. When they were halfway across town with the load of hay, the axle broke on the trailer.

"Shoot!" Eddy says, "I have a date with Mim in two hours."

"What should we do?" my brother asks.

"No time to fix the thing. Let's get the Ranchero and move the bales a few at a time."

He unhooks the trailer, leaving it loaded with hay by the side of the road. They drive the tractor to the farm where he keeps his sheep, get into his Ranchero, drive back to the trailer and load as many bales as they can fit onto the truck bed, then drive back to the farm and unload. Eddy remains calm, as he and Arthur work as quickly as they can. They repeat the same procedure until all sixty bales are moved. Afterward, Eddy sighs, and says, "I barely have time to get ready to pick up Mim." He looks at my brother, thinking, then adds, "Will you wash my car while I get ready? I'll pay you, then I'll drop you at home on my way to pick her up."

"Sure," says Arthur, who was twelve, and anxious to earn the extra money. Eddy managed to get to Maryanne's without being late.

It was a fall morning at the high school during my sophomore year, when a buzz went around campus. Everyone was talking about it. On the hill behind the school there were two giant letters which could be seen all over town—SL for San Luis. Someone had changed it to say AG, for the Arroyo Grande team our football team was to play Friday night. Blood was boiling, tempers were flaring. Everyone was saying, "How could they?" or "We'll get them." The football players were enraged. That night, a car full of football players drove to the Arroyo Grande campus with some diesel fuel and used it to write SL on their football field. After a quick investigation, it turned out that nobody from Arroyo Grande had committed this crime against our school. Our football players decided it must have been Mission High, our rival school across town. Armed with paint, they raced to Mission's football field, and painted everywhere, in the bathrooms, on the grass, making a mess. It was determined that nobody from Mission had tampered with our SL either. Our football players were in a heap of trouble for all the damage they had done, and nobody ever figured out who had changed our SL to AG.

As far as I know, nobody ever learned who did it. Except me. I found out, but it was forty-five years later. I discovered it was Eddy, who was under the influence of his friend Tom St. John in much the same way that Huckleberry Finn would influence Tom Sawyer. Tom claims to be the instigator, and he liked getting Eddy to do things to break out of his comfort zone. Besides, Tom was mischievous and Eddy was his best friend and he wanted company on his escapades. They did the fair stuff together, and hauled hay together, usually making one dollar a bale. And they went out in the middle of one dark night, climbed that hill, and turned the SL into an AG. Nobody ever suspected, nor ever would suspect, the unassuming, shy Edward August Schultz, FFA president, the church-going, quiet young man.

I saw Eddy a lot at school that year because our lockers were close, but it's no wonder I didn't see him much at home and after school because besides raising forty sheep and a steer, he was on the FFA parliamentary procedures team and on the track team. He was either practicing for competitions or track meets, or he was at them. His parliamentary procedures team earned second place in the state competition. I don't know how he had time to date Maryanne, but he squeezed it in somehow and continued to work at Madonna Inn. He accomplished so much in the same amount of time that everyone else had, but I can't remember one time in my life seeing him frazzled or in a rush. He managed to do everything with the inner peace of a monk.

My family and Grandma, Grandpa and Sandy went to Eddy's high school graduation in June 1965. We have a home movie taken after the ceremony. He's in front of the gym at Cal Poly, wearing the blue graduation gown, smiling and holding Karen, who is almost three. There are scenes in the movie after graduation in the yard at his home. In one, he's squatting down next to Karen, and I'm on the other side of her. We're both telling her to look at the camera and to wave. Eddy's smile is contagious as he looks into the camera. The next shot is of him getting into his Pontiac with his graduation gown hanging at the back window. He drives away from the house with a smile that tells of a happy heart. He was on his way to pick up Maryanne to take her to Grad Night.

The Marines were the first combat troops sent to Vietnam. They were sent to Da Nang in March of 1965, when we still had never heard of Vietnam. They increased the numbers of troops rapidly after that. On July 28th, President Johnson announced the draft would increase from 17,000 soldiers a month to 35,000 a month, satisfying a request by General Westmoreland. By fall, there were 155,000 American troops in Vietnam. At the end of 1965, there were 200,000. In 1966, the number doubled to 400,000. Americans were beginning to hear about a little strip of land called Vietnam. But it seemed a world far away to me.

Maryanne's dad hired Eddy and Tom to stack hay for two dollars per bale (double what they were usually paid) that summer of 1965. They lifted each bale using the tractor, then dropped it onto the stacks of hay in the barn. At Tom's mischievous suggestion, they took to playing a reckless game. They took turns lying on the stack of hay, moving out of the way just in time before the next bale was dropped. You had to be quick. It was Tom's turn to lie on the bales. The rope snapped on the bale being dropped. Tom moved out of the way fast, but got his leg stuck between two bales and fell sideways. He avoided the bale falling on him but he slammed into a hay hook, which pierced his head. He got up, not clear what had happened, numb and not feeling the pain at first. The first thing he saw when he stood up was Eddy's face, which had gone white. Eddy stared in disbelief at his friend who had a hay hook stuck in his head. Dazed, Eddy managed to get Tom to his Ranchero and then sped him to the hospital. This was long before cell phones so he wasn't able to call 911. Tom lived through the ordeal, to tell the story many a time.

Tom might have inspired Eddy to do a few pranks, have a few beers, and be a bit too daring, but Eddy was a good guy, with a good heart, and I can't think of a person who would have said one negative thing about him; he was well-liked by all. It was about this time when someone close to us had taken up smoking. Eddy talked to me about it and was adamant that he would never, ever smoke.

August fair time arrived. Eddy and Maryanne spent as much time together as they could, though they were both busy with their fair chores and animals. It was Eddy's busiest year in FFA. He showed ewes and rams in several breeding classes, and he also showed a replacement heifer, and a steer. Even after years of practice, there was an element of nervousness before going into the ring. In the holding pen, waiting to go into the ring, he would take a deep breath and most likely, say a prayer, because he was quietly close to God in all he did. Maryanne took a lamb for the first time, and he showed her how to sheer it, and to show it. Eddy knew he was going to miss showing animals. From FFA, he had learned a lot, and gained a lot of experience, and all of it would propel him toward his future—to become the manager of a large ranch, just like he'd told me when he was a boy.

After high school, Eddy attended Cuesta Junior College, which, in those days, was held in old National Guard barracks located at Camp San Luis at the base of Bishop Peak, which was one of the nine sister peaks that stand in a row, like guardians pointing the way from the ocean in Morro Bay into the town of San Luis Obispo. The ceilings of the crumbling barracks leaked like a faucet when it rained, so students shared classrooms with puddles of water. Wind blew through the cracks and holes in the walls so you had to wear a jacket inside during winter months. I started there two years later and it was exactly the same. We might as well have been taking classes in the outdoors. Eddy was on the wrestling team at Cuesta and his coach, Warren Hansen, said Eddy was the hardest worker on the team, was always first in the training runs and he always made his weight class, never letting his team or the coach down. Coach Hansen awarded him the Most Inspirational Wrestler award in 1966. I didn't go to too many of his functions because I was busy with my own stuff, but I went to at least one of the Cuesta wrestling matches with the family and in addition to the musty smell of the gym, I remember Grandpa beaming with pride.

During the summer of 1966, Eddy worked long hard hours hauling hay for local ranchers with his friend Steve Boyle. It was an unbearably hot day in June when Eddy told Steve, "It's your birthday. I'll finish the last two loads by myself as your present." It was hard work on a hot day and Steve never forgot what a huge gift that was.

Eddy and Maryanne spent every Sunday together, going to Walther League events, or driving to their leadership meetings. They packed in a lot of activities, as much as they could, because she'd be leaving for college before long. They went to her high school prom, and suddenly it was time for Grad Night. After the fair of 1966, when they both showed animals again, Maryanne had to leave for college, to a Lutheran University in another state. It was a difficult farewell, knowing that, except for the two weeks she would be home for Christmas, she would be gone for nine months.

Eddy, Grandma, Grandpa, Dad and Karen, Mom, Judy, me,
Sandy, Arthur in front with our dog, Shadow; 1962.

Mom, Grandpa, Gary, Grandma, Carl, Sandy, Eddy;
December 1967.

Eddy working on an FFA project on Laurel Lane; 1964.

Eddy's graduation picture; 1965.

My graduation picture; 1967.

Chapter Ten
Fellow Comrade

Vietnam
1965–1966

The boy isn't a boy anymore. He's a young adult and he's been a Viet Cong soldier for seven years. He fell in love with a fellow comrade, a woman two years his senior. They shared secrets and plans for the future. They had hopes that the north and south would be one, ruled by the same government, the communist government, and there would be no more war. By 1965, the Viet Cong had destroyed over 7,000 villages in South Vietnam. He didn't like war, but it was all he'd known. He liked being on the side of power. He was a survivor and he aimed to survive.

Everywhere he turned there were Americans lurking in the jungle that was his home. There was nothing he wanted more than for the Americans to leave, to let his country be, and to let the north and the south become one. There was a day he will never forget, a day when time seemed to stop. He was with the woman he planned to marry, his fellow soldier. They were in the jungle. An American B-52 flew 2000 feet above, which was a common occurrence. Suddenly a bomb dropped. He shouted at her to run. She ran the wrong way. The bomb hit her and he witnessed the woman he loved, the only joy in his life, disappear before his eyes into a hail of body parts. He wished it had been him instead. His heart was crushed as if the bomb had hit him. Living is worse than dying he realized. But for whatever reason, he was a survivor. He didn't know why.

Chapter Eleven
Anti-War Protests

California
1967

In 1967, the world seemed to change overnight. It was like watching one of those films that time-lapse the growth of a flower. All of a sudden there are hippies, peace signs and young people wearing flowers, headbands and beads. Guys who wore crew cuts and buzzes their whole lives let their hair grow, some down to their waist. Two years before, you never saw a guy with long hair. The world transformed like a cocoon into a butterfly and, much like the cocoon, it had been brewing for some time. The volatile political scene evolved from a war in Vietnam that had been simmering since 1954 and then converged with a generation of youth who were coming of age, the Baby Boomers, who had grown out of the child-centered environment of the fifties and burst full force into the hippie movement. For the Baby Boomers born in 1949, which included me, who were starting college that year, it was a time of turmoil, unrest, and was drastically different from only a couple of years before.

The draft board again escalated their numbers, so that by 1967, the draft was affecting everyone and people were not complacent about it. Vietnam was no longer a tiny country that nobody had heard of. It became the most talked about subject. It was like an infestation of rattle snakes and you didn't know who was going to get bit.

Young men, ages eighteen through twenty-six, were given pre-induction physical exams to receive classification of 1A (fit for draft) or 4F (unfit for draft). All families, including ours, felt in the midst of a game of Russian roulette. Eddy was classified as 1A. If it didn't end, Arthur, my brother, who was fifteen, would also be involved. Was it just a matter of time?

It was around this time that I had a boyfriend who didn't pass Eddy's inspection.

"Hey Lynne," he says one evening after having dinner at our house, "that guy you're seeing, he's not a good choice."

"Why?" I asked.

"He's just not good. You can't trust him."

"How do you know?"

"I just know. Maryanne feels the same way. She had a class with him last year, saw how he was, heard things he said. He's arrogant, and not to be trusted."

I should have broken up with my boyfriend immediately, but I remembered Eddy's words, and before long I learned Eddy was right. I was glad he was there to give me relationship advice, to watch out for me, like he had always done.

Eddy continued to bale hay and wait tables at Madonna Inn. He loved to tell about the night Mama Cass from the famous singing group, The Mamas and Papas, came in and he waited on her. He was one of the hardest working people I ever knew, and the kindest. His ever present quick and easy smile welcomed you like a morning cup of hot coffee and must have earned him a lot of tips at the restaurant.

On July 15th, a month after I graduated from high school, Sandy married Sal Melendez in the Catholic Church in San Luis Obispo. Judy and I were bridesmaids and Eddy was an usher. Sandy met Sal after she returned from working in Yosemite. She worked in the cafeteria at Cal Poly where he was an architecture student. He passed through the food line every day, partly because she had caught his eye. She liked Sal Mineo, the actor, so I don't know if she liked Sal Mineo because of Sal or if it was the other way around, but for whatever reason they found each other, fell in love and are still married today. Sal received a draft notice not long before the wedding, ordering him to report for duty prior to his wedding, so he made a choice to enlist in order to get some time to be able to go through with the wedding.

Eddy had also received a draft notice. He stared at it. He would have to drop out of college. He would have to be even further away from Maryanne. What about his sheep? His cars? His life would have to go on hold. He made out the words; it said to report to the bus depot in San Luis Obispo on August 1st. He would be allowed to come home for a brief period after the training and before reporting to wherever he would have to serve. Most likely it would be Vietnam, as that's where most draftees were sent. Without a complaint to anyone he quit school, quit his job, and figured out what to do with his sheep and his cars.

Before his report date, Eddy drove his new brother-in-law, Sal, to the Los Angeles Induction Center, where Sal was inducted before he headed to basic training at Fort Ord, California, and then on to a base in Germany where he would be stationed for nearly three years and Sandy would join him. On the road to Los Angeles with Sal, Eddy explained to him that he didn't want to enlist and give the three years. This way he would be done in two years, and back to pursuing his goal of running a ranch.

After returning from taking Sal, he prepared to leave and said his good-byes. The Greyhound bus depot on August 1st was crowded with young men, barely grown, who had been plucked from their secure homes, their jobs, their schools, and for many it was their first time away from home. It was a long ride to Los Angeles with most of them deep in thought about what was in store. There were a few who brought beer, drank it and got sick, causing the bus driver to pull over twice for puking teens. I'm certain Eddy remained calm in the midst of the chaos, because that's who he was. Upon arrival, they were put in a decrepit hotel in central Los Angeles. It groaned from the activity of hundreds of teenagers and young men from all over California. The draftees ran with unruly abandon up and down the wide corridors, so that with its moaning floors and menacing ancient walls, the hotel became a prison of trapped teens forced into a terrifying nightmarish future. Toilet paper rolls were thrown out upper story windows, becoming ghostlike streamers as they unrolled on the way down. One frustrated teen threw a TV out the seventh story window. These boys had grown up in the fifties, a time of peace and plenty. Most of their mothers didn't work, and had been there for them with cookies from the oven when they came home from school. These barely raised young men were put in rooms alphabetically, so Eddy shared a room with David Stafford, whom he had gone to high school with. Both of them had been attending junior college when the notice came that ripped them from their lives.

David's parents were on a two-week vacation when he received the notice ordering him to the bus depot. Just like Eddy, he thought about his job, his college classes, his girlfriend, and his apartment he had recently moved into, and that his parents were on a trip to Canada. His girlfriend was on vacation with her family. It didn't feel right, but he had to act quickly in order to be at the bus depot to leave on the first of August, so in a stunned manner, he did what he had to do. He packed his things into boxes and unloaded them into his parent's living room. He wrote them a note that he was drafted, taped it to one of the boxes, and went to the bus depot. He didn't get to say goodbye to his parents or his girlfriend, or even tell them he was leaving because it was the world before cell phones, email, and texting; you couldn't reach people instantly. He didn't even know exactly where they were on their trip, or how to contact them. He learned later of his mother's tears when she arrived home to find their son's boxes and his note, their world changed—their son seized from his life and taken from them before they could say good-bye.

That first night in Los Angeles, in that run-down 1930s hotel, the noise in the hallways from wild boys on the loose went on for most of the night, but Eddy and David sat on their beds and held a quiet conversation talking of the war, and what it meant to them.

"I'm going to do what I'm called on to do, and do it the best that I can," said Eddy.

"Me too," said David, "all we can do is to give our best. Duty calls." They both had a mature outlook, without anger like some of the others. It's not what either wanted and they were scared, but the two of them decided to confront it with dedication. David couldn't sleep all night and in the middle of the night he walked outside and found a run-down theatre where he watched a movie, which helped keep his fears at bay. Eddy slept soundly.

After a long, grueling day of being shuttled along, and treated like cattle as they were given physicals, most of them felt dehumanized. After the second night, they were sent to basic training, some to Fort Bliss, Texas, like Eddy and David. Once they arrived in Fort Bliss they were in separate parts of the huge base and had no contact again.

After Fort Bliss, Eddy was sent to Fort Polk, Louisiana for eight weeks of Advanced Individual Training (AIT) in combat guerilla warfare exercises.

During his training, from August until December 1967, anti-war movements were as popular as star athletes. Approximately 4,000 protesters showed up in Oakland and blocked busloads of draftees from reaching the Induction Center. It made the headlines because there were over a hundred arrests, including that of the famous folk singer, Joan Baez. The police caused injury to many by throwing stun grenades into the angry crowd and also shooting them with rubber pellets. At the Lincoln Memorial, a larger group of 70,000–100,000 objectors demonstrated on October 21st; over 600 were arrested. They marched from there to the Pentagon, wearing headbands, beads, flowers, bell bottoms, and long hair. Peace symbols were painted on clothes, cars, signs and worn around the neck as jewelry. Homemade signs of all shapes and sizes cried out, "Make love not war!" Draft cards burned, crumbling into falling ash.

In November 1967, there had been approximately 11,000 deaths of United States soldiers in Vietnam. The bombing of North Vietnam continued to escalate.

Every day, accounts and pictures of protesters permeated the news on TV and in the newspapers. In December, there was a *Stop the Draft Week* at the Army Induction Center in New York. Like the other gatherings, the colorful demonstrators chanted angry protests while waving signs and posters that screamed of outrage. Police arrested more than 500, including the famous pediatrician, Dr. Benjamin Spock and also Allen Ginsberg who was a well-known, outspoken poet. It was a kaleidoscope-colored week, with peace signs, flowers, beads, long hair, bright colors, and tie-dyed clothes. Scenes were blasted across the news, but it seemed remote from me. I watched the news, saw the demonstrations, but the protestors seemed as far away as the war itself because none of it occurred in our town of San Luis Obispo which, in those days, had a population of around 15,000. I was against the war, against the draft, but I didn't participate because it was far from us, and I was studying for my college classes, working at Arctic Circle (a local hamburger stand that is now called Frank's), spending time with friends, dating, and going to the beach. Though I agreed with the war protest, I didn't agree with the cruelty toward soldiers, which was happening to those who returned after a year of fighting in the gruesome war and giving up a year of their lives to do it. They were being spit on and attacked by anti-war demonstrators and hippies. It was cruel, wrong and I felt they were contradicting themselves. They demonstrated against the draft, then spit on the ones who returned after being drafted. It seemed hypocritical. It made them appear self-centered. They were against the draft because they didn't want to be drafted themselves, but the ones who were, and returned, were mocked and degraded. The anger should have been only toward the government, not toward the draftees who were forced to give up a year of their lives. Not to mention the ones who lost their lives.

It was a world after President Kennedy was assassinated but before his brother, Bobby, was. It was before Martin Luther King's assassination; his speeches against the war were on TV. *Light My Fire, By the Time I Get to Phoenix, To Sir with Love,* and *White Rabbit* were popular songs of the day. The movies, *The Graduate, The Dirty Dozen,* and *The Great Escape* were hits. The hippie movement set the fashion style of the times and that did hit our town, even if the demonstrations didn't. Teens across the nation wore brightly colored flowered bell bottoms and Army surplus clothing. I wasn't a hippie but I wore the style of the era, the flowered bell bottoms and the long straight hair, as did my friends and peers.

On November 9th, 1967, the first photos of the entire earth were taken from the unmanned Apollo 4. It showed a peaceful picture of our planet Earth traveling through space, with nothing in the picture to show the violence, the war, the crime of man against man, or the fact that thousands of our young men were taken from their homes and sent to kill their fellow travelers on planet Earth. It's a peaceful, beautiful ball of blue and green floating in space, as if there were no such thing as war.

Eddy returned before Christmas and had two weeks before leaving for Vietnam. Grandma and Grandpa had a family dinner the night he came home and I didn't go because I already had plans with friends, which I'm ashamed to admit.

The next morning I was at Cuesta, the junior college, where I was a student and where Eddy had been going before he was drafted. I walked down the center aisle of the cafeteria toward the snack bar, not noticing the lone fellow at the table to my right. When I think of that day, time stops. It's as vivid as the brightest full arching rainbow I'd ever seen.

"Lynne!" he calls. It still echoes in my brain.

I glance that way, and there's Eddy sitting alone at one of the long tables. "How come you didn't come to dinner last night?" he asks. It's my first time to see him in four months, since he left in August, and my heart leapt with joy at seeing him. He'd never been away before and it had seemed so long.

"I'm sorry. I should have been there," I say, as I slide in across from him. "I already had plans. I should have cancelled but I knew I would see you sometime today and all week."

Then I notice. He's smoking. "Why are you smoking? You said you would never, ever smoke! You were adamant about it."

"Boot camp was tough, really tough, and I needed it. It helped me relax. It was the only way to get relief. Want to see my dog tags?"

"Sure, what are dog tags?" I was more naive than I like to admit.

He pulls them from around his neck. I hold them, turn them over and inspect them. "It's got all your information on it in case you die," he says.

Suddenly the cacophony of students talking, filling up other tables and walking in and out, fades away like background in a movie close-up scene. The moment stands alone, it is still. It *is* a close-up scene. It's like another time, another place, to see Eddy smoking and talking about if he were to die. It's just the two of us at that table but in that moment I feel like there is nobody but us in the room, nobody but us in the world, as we ponder the gravity of the meaning of dog tags. He's twenty-one. I'm eighteen. *I am holding his dog tags.* My entire life had held Eddy in it. He was three when I was born. He is talking of dying and we are sitting in a college cafeteria where he should still be going to school, with a lifetime ahead of him. As I look at the dog tags, then glance at his face, and see him smoking, I know that I will never forget the poignancy of the moment, nor will I forget, never in a million years will I forget, the change in his eyes. They aren't the soft, happy eyes of "The Kid," the sweet church-going boy, the laughing, kind child with a worthwhile goal of becoming a rancher, the boy they called, "Daddy's Tail." Nor do they seem angry or filled with resentment. Instead, his eyes are flooded with a somber knowledge that tells me without words that he has glimpsed his future. The change in him is subtle but I detect it. He now knows things that I do not. This time, they are things he cannot, or will not, teach me.

A few days later, on Sunday, December 17th, we are at Great Grandma Schultz's (Eddy's Grandma's) in Arroyo Grande, for an early Christmas celebration. Every year she and my great Aunt Lucille, who lives with her, have a family open house with lots of food to celebrate. I'd been thinking about the subtle change I'd seen in Eddy and I'm now scared about him going to war, which had previously seemed remote. The reality is sinking into my brain. The house is swarming with relatives in every room. There are so many. My grandpa is one of six kids and the house is filled with many of his siblings and in-laws, plus their children and grandchildren as well as many of his own. People are talking, laughing, and celebrating the holiday season. Often Eddy and I find each other during times like this, as if we are kindred spirits. He's dressed for Christmas in a collared, plaid, button-up shirt, with a white T-shirt underneath. We are standing near the doorway between the living room and the hallway, and I ask, "Are you scared?"

"No," he says, pauses, then adds, "More people are killed on freeways than in Vietnam." I think he's trying to convince me, but maybe trying to convince himself also.

"Is that true?"

"Yep, it's true. It's going to be ok. I'll be back." He seems more confident today, and I believe him.

Karen joins us. She's five now, and understands he's leaving, but doesn't understand much about war, not that I have a grasp on it either. She's in her pretty pink party dress, with her blonde, straight hair hanging to her shoulders and a small pony tail tied from the top over to the side. He looks at her with love and that peaceful, almost saintly, look of his, and says, "You take care of Cayenne for me, okay?" Cayenne had been an untrained yearling, but Grandpa and Eddy worked with him, using a hackamore, until he finally accepted a saddle and Eddy was able to ride him.

"I will," she says, proudly.

"And when I come back I'll teach you to ride him." Karen takes that promise to her heart.

On Christmas day, our family gathers at Grandma and Grandpa's. Grandpa had enclosed a huge porch making it into a family room. Two long tables are set up for the Christmas meal. My cousins Linda, Danny and Richard (Uncle Gary's kids), and John, Mike, Mark and Sammy (Uncle Carl's kids) and me, Judy, Arthur and Karen are sitting around the kid's table. Eddy graduated to the adult table this year because he's going off to war. Sandy, at twenty-three, has also been at the adult table for a couple of years. Uncle Gary asks Eddy about his basic training and my cousin, Linda, age fourteen, hears Eddy say how mean the sergeants are, that one of them hit him in the head with the butt of a rifle when he looked the wrong direction. Eddy is the nicest person anyone could ever know and to hear that somebody did that to him is more than disturbing.

Maryanne is home from college for Christmas break, so she and Eddy see each other often, making up for their separation. Eddy missed her a lot, especially with what he went through in basic training. He takes her out on Christmas night, after our family celebration. He asks her to marry him when he returns from Vietnam. She replies, "Yes! Yes, yes!"

Before long, it's the night before he leaves and he comes to our house for dinner. I'm having trouble believing he'll be gone in the morning, and for a whole year. After dinner, I have to leave because I have a date who arrives to pick me up. I wonder why I accepted a date on Eddy's last night but I find out later that he went out with friends that night and wouldn't have hung out with us all evening anyway. Eddy and I stand face to face. He's next to the fireplace, resting his elbow on the mantle, with his face resting in his hand, staring at me. I'm looking at him too. Neither of us have words. A year seems like a century. I know I won't forget this moment, as I try to memorize his face. I will never forget his eyes; they tell more than I want to know. They permeate with a silent, deeper sense of destiny, a loss of innocence. How is it that eyes can say so much without talking? Mom stands next to me and she breaks the silence by saying, "Well, aren't you two going to kiss goodbye?"

With both of us as shy as we are, we get embarrassed and I say, "Oh, Mom." We hug and say our good-byes, leaving out the kiss because it felt awkward. He says, "I'll see you in a year." With his face and his words imprinted in my brain, I turn to leave, believing him. Believing him, because he said so.

Edward August Schultz, military picture; 1967.

Chapter Twelve
The War

Vietnam
1968

It was January 1968. The morning after Eddy came to dinner, he rode a bus for four hours to the Armed Forces Induction Center in Oakland where he would prepare to join the nearly 500,000 U.S. troops already in Vietnam.

On the morning he flew out, he was on guard duty and missed formation. He made it up later which gave him no time to call home to say good-bye before boarding on the Continental Airline flight for Vietnam. We didn't have cell phones, email or Facebook for fast communication in those days. My grandparents didn't hear from him until they received this postcard through the military mail (therefore no postage stamp):

Used to the golden, dry hills of California, he thought the lush forests of the Philippines and the seas were so beautiful that he took a whole roll of pictures. He took a couple of pictures of the Bataan Peninsula where the World War II Bataan Death March had occurred. At the end of his final flight he landed at Bien Hoa Air Base, twenty-two miles northeast of Saigon (called Ho Chi Minh City today).

From Bien Hoa Air Base, Eddy loaded into a bus with other young soldiers, all, most likely, wondering about their destiny, as they traveled over a hot, dusty red road to Cu Chi, about seven miles north of the air base. He would have to get used the heat and the dirt. In his first letter to Grandma and Grandpa, Eddy wrote:

Dear Mom & Dad,

I got here at I don't know what time. I'm about a ½ day ahead of you. I've processed in the country here but haven't been sent to my unit yet so I still don't know what my address is or what unit I'll be in. This place has definite disadvantages. It's real dusty here and everything is dirty. The expected high for today is 90 degrees which is a little warm for me. I guess I could get a pretty good tan here.

We changed our money too. The money we use now is like Monopoly money. Small change is paper money. The $10 bills are the same size as our regular bills. I should have a permanent address in 3 or 4 days. We have a TV station here and 2 or 3 radio stations. We don't have every modern *convenience we had back in the states though. Our shower room works by centrifugal force I guess. There's a high water tower and pipes that run down into the shower room. I'm going to chow now.*

Love, Ed

Eddy was assigned to the 25th Infantry Division, headquartered at Cu Chi. When he and the other draftees stepped off the bus, the place was swarming with truckloads of soldiers coming and going in every direction, as busy as an ant colony. There were soldiers everywhere, tanks, cannons, trucks and a constant roar of helicopters overhead. It was like a major city, except everything was a dusty olive green, and it was all about war. He was immediately issued field gear: mosquito nets, ponchos, plastic canteens, ammo and an M-16 rifle. The heat and humidity were intense, and dust stuck to his sweat the way a fly sticks to flypaper. He'd grown up in the mild weather of California's central coast so this would take some getting used to.

Eddy received orientation and fitness training in Cu Chi for five days before being sent to base camp. On the fourth night, while watching a movie, a siren blasted, startling him like a clap of thunder might do. It was a mortar attack (cannon projectiles) by the Viet Cong. Troops were running everywhere. The siren and chaos lasted for a half hour. One of the theatres across the base had been hit. Two soldiers were killed. Eddy and the other guys went back to watching their movie but it was hard to keep their minds on the movie. God was always by Eddy's side, even in the middle of a war zone, and this was a time for prayer.

Here are excerpts from Eddy's second letter to my grandparents, dated Jan. 14th, 1968:

Dear Mom & Dad,

I'm in Cu Chi now. It's the headquarters of the 25th Infantry Division, which I was assigned to. I start my schooling tomorrow. We were issued our field gear yesterday and our M-K today. By the way, I guess you have noticed by my address I'm a PFC. Maybe I can come home a sergeant.

I make a little better than $8 overseas pay, $65 hazardous duty pay and my base pay; it adds up to almost $200. They take out for Social Security and my bond so I'm sending $120 home to start with, that will leave me with $60.

There are some of my army clothes being sent home that I turned in at Oakland and a couple days ago I sent $100 home.

The only time I might need a lot of money will be when I go on R&R, then I'll probably send home for some. Let me know how everything is at home. Did Johnny Hopkins [his cousin] call about the car? I didn't figure he would, but just wondered if I could be wrong.

Love, Eddy

It was January 19th, his mother's birthday, and it was three days after his father's birthday, when he was airlifted to what he thought would be his home away from home, his base camp at Dau Tieng, thirty-five kilometers (about twenty-two miles) northwest of Cu Chi. It was his first helicopter ride in his twenty-one-year-old life, and though the cooling effect of the warm wind blowing through the open door was pleasant, he and the other soldiers on board knew the reality of war was before them. From the air, they could see that Dau Tieng was smaller than Cu Chi, but still bounding with the activity of soldiers moving here and there in dusty, dark green Army trucks and tanks, and of shirtless, sweaty soldiers digging trenches for protection. It looked as busy as a bee hive and reminiscent of the miniature worlds we used to create in the dirt on the farm. In the middle of the base there was a swimming pool. It was from a previous life when Vietnam was occupied by France and Dau Tieng had been a French resort. When the Huey hovered close to the ground, Eddy and the others jumped out and dashed out of the way of the rotor blades. One of the first things they noticed was the smell. It was humid, but mixed with sweat, dust and they didn't know what else. The chop-chop sound of helicopters was unrelenting. Hueys and Cobras were landing and taking off constantly. The unpaved chopper landing zone was next to Eddy's barrack, so as he was shown his sleeping quarters, a circle of red dust drifted through the air and pushed its way through the screen window into his quarters, giving everything in the room a reddish, dusty covering, including the soldiers themselves.

The mortar attack at Cu Chi was a preview of what would be almost a daily occurrence at Dau Tieng. The Viet

Cong were on the attack, aiming to destroy Dau Tieng because its purpose was to block the Viet Cong's supply route (the Ho Chi Min Trail) from Cambodia to South Vietnam. I have a friend who was a transport pilot in Vietnam in the early 1960s and his comment was that we could have easily bombed and destroyed the Viet Cong's access on that trail, and he never understood why it was not ordered. Instead, the ground troops were sent in to try to block the trail. Day and night there existed a constant roar of cannons and artillery.

The one benefit of the base at Dau Tieng was that it was located at the southern edge of the Michelin Rubber Plantation (which covered 31,000 acres), and parts of camp were shaded by fifty-foot-tall rubber trees. Though the trees were tall and thin, they branched out at the top, with lots of wide leaves, creating a green canopy. Toward the north, there was a view of the Black Virgin Mountain, a cone shaped extinct volcano, which stood 3,000 feet above the Tay Ninh Valley.

Eddy's platoon and most of his company were not in Dau Tieng when he arrived. A major battle had taken place at Fire Support Base Burt, which was 33 km (20.5 miles) north, near the Cambodian border. The battle, which was called the Battle of Soui Cut, took place on January 1st and 2nd, 1968, while Eddy was in Oakland preparing for his departure. His platoon and company had been sent to Fire Support Base Burt to do sweeps and security after that major battle had ended. This battle had the 2nd largest enemy loss in the war, with approximately 400 enemy lives lost. This intense battle was depicted in the movie, *Platoon*, as told by its director, Oliver Stone, who had been one of the soldiers involved.

A sergeant handed Eddy and the other new guys each a beer (covered in dust). Eddy learned there were 133 men in his company (Charlie Company) and 24 men in his platoon, the 2nd Platoon of the 2nd Battalion, 12th Infantry, 25th Infantry Division. He was told that when his time came to go into "the field" he might not get back to base camp for six or seven months. So much for thinking this was his home away from home. There was outgoing mortar that first night across the dirt road from his barrack, and it nearly shook him right out of his cot—his welcome into the world of war. A mild welcome compared to what was to come.

He wrote home that night, Jan. 19th:

Dear Mom and Dad,

Happy Birthday to both of you. I'm sorry I can't get you anything, but it is hard to send things when you're not at a permanent camp, and it takes a long time to get something to the states.

I'm at my base camp in Dau Tieng. We got in here today. The monsoon season will start around May. From what I hear that is the best time of the year. It's cooler in both ways. We can't do too many operations at that time of year.

Oh, I forgot to tell you the main reason you're only getting a letter for your birthdays is I almost forgot them; I guess you probably guessed that though. I am sending that roll of colored film home. I got a little carried away over the

Philippines and used up all 12 pictures there. I finally found some more film but it's black and white. It's hard to get colored film here. I'll take some pictures of my base camp here and send these pictures home. I don't know if it would be too smart to take my camera out in the field.

I've got my rifle and 140 rounds of ammo right by my bed here. Any time we have a mortar attack I grab my steel pot (helmet), rifle and ammo and head for the bunker. I'm nowhere near where they fire the mortars at. They try for headquarters and the airport and C Company is on the other side of the base from them.

After 90 days I'm eligible to put in for R&R. I haven't decided where to go yet, but I have plenty of time. We are eligible for one out of country R&R, one in country R&R and one 7 day leave. I might get out early when I come home too. Since it will be so close to Christmas. I came over at a good time of the year and got in a good company.

We're treated like equals here almost. Quite a change from AIT and Basic.

I hope you both had a happy birthday and I'll keep you posted on things in this dust bowl.

Love, Eddy

A week later, on January 26th, Eddy's company returned from Fire Support Base Burt and he met Andy Wahrenbrock and the rest of his platoon. Andy, who was tall and lanky, was from West Covina, in the Los Angeles area, which was a three hour drive from San Luis Obispo. Eddy and Andy hit it off and became best friends. Maybe it was because they were both from California, maybe because they both had quick smiles and easy-going personalities or maybe because Eddy was the RTO (radio operator), and Andy was the medic, which required them to stay together at all times. Perhaps it was all three reasons that they became buddies living through a hellish time together, day and night in the trenches in the middle of a war zone.

He also met Jerry Counts and Robert Coulter that day. They were two draftees who had both grown up in Irving, Texas, a small farming town. Because their last names were alphabetically close they were drafted at the same time, sent to basic training together, then put in the same platoon in Vietnam. Jerry, who had a boyish face, looking younger than his twenty years, liked to tell about the day he and Robert flew in to Vietnam. From the air, Robert, age twenty-one, looked out the window to the ground below and saw huge water-filled pits in the earth and in his thick, Texan drawl, said, "Look at all the stock tanks!" thinking they were water tanks for thirsty cattle. Little did he know that the holes were bomb craters that had filled with monsoon rain water, and in the near future he'd be using them to bathe. When these two Texas farm boys landed, as they got off the plane, Jerry said to Robert, also in his Texan accent, "I ain't killin' anybody." And Robert replied, "I ain't killin' anybody either!"

Dave Glass, from Minnesota, was a tall, dark-haired sergeant who liked to talk and took pride in what he did. He was clever and, though young, figured out how to do everything he needed to do with skill and ease. He had been wounded from battle in November and spent time in base camp healing, but he was back in the field and had just returned with the rest of them from Fire Support Base Burt, after Eddy had arrived. He often acted as platoon sergeant, second in command.

Lorence (Larry) Lundby, from Waterloo, Iowa, was fondly called "Lumpy" by his platoon brothers. He was a twenty-six year old draftee who had been "in country" six months and who went out one night on his R&R, got drunk and married a local Vietnamese girl whom he'd never met before.

Jerry Miller, a friendly, smart young man from North Carolina, had been in Vietnam for a few months, along with Dave. He was made sergeant within a couple of months. He and Dave alternated acting as platoon sergeant, second in command under the platoon leader.

The platoon leader was Harold Steele from South Carolina, a platoon sergeant acting as platoon leader because they had no lieutenant to fill the job at the time. A veteran of WWII and Korea, he was a true soldier in the eyes of these young draftees who were mostly between nineteen and twenty-two years old. They called him "Pappy Steele" because, at nearly forty, he seemed old from their youthful perspectives. He was a small-framed man, but could carry another's load in addition to his own if need be. He was always there for his troops and they loved and respected him.

These men would become the constants in Eddy's life, the ones he would count on, the ones he would share things with; they would be together day and night in the midst of constant danger; they would become his family.

Andy Wahrenbrock, the medic; 1968.

Robert Coulter and Jerry Counts, both from Texas;
1968.

Andy Wahrenbrock.   Eddy took this of his base camp.

Dave Glass from Minnesota.   Members of Eddy's
platoon; March 1968.

Chapter Thirteen
Cookies

California
1968

At home, there is little complacency in this time of the increasing draft. Young adults are charged, ready for action, like subatomic particles. Passion mixed with outrage electrifies the air. Anti-war activists are trying to get the Peace and Freedom Party on the ballot. Peace signs are everywhere: on shirts, windows, cars, signs, jewelry. Teenagers are running off to compounds or living on Haight and Ashbury Streets in San Francisco, becoming hippies overnight. Guys are letting their hair grow and girls are going braless. The news on TV and radio is all about the Vietnam War, and the protests against it. Many college students demonstrate, but only at the risk of losing their college deferments. The world of 1968 suddenly seems a crazy place and is unrecognizable from the world of 1965.

Grandpa buys a '55 tan Mercedes to restore as a surprise for Eddy when he returns. I think it gives him something to focus on, to think positively about Eddy returning. It was hard on Grandpa with Eddy gone. One of Grandpa's other sons, Carl, was in World War II, and returned unscathed, and now Grandpa has to live through the same worry again with his youngest son, and this one, his baby, his little shadow. Grandpa never had to go to war. He was too young for World War I, and too old for World War II, so war was an unknown to him. However, his baby brother came home from the Battle of the Bulge during WWII with a hand shot off. So Grandpa is well aware of the dangers and he watches the news and reads the paper every day, scrutinizing every report.

I make a batch of chocolate chip cookies, pack them in a three pound coffee can and Judy draws a picture and sticks it into the can. We wrap it securely and take it to the post office. I write a letter telling him cookies are on the way and I mail it separately, knowing the cookies will take much longer to reach him. We're all on pins and needles to hear from him. When a letter comes, news spreads through the family like wildfire. It takes a couple of weeks for letters to arrive, so all of his news is old news. But we live for word no matter how delayed the letter. The following letter was written at the end of January, when they came in from the field because of Tet, which stands for Tet Nguyen Dan, which is the first day of the Vietnamese lunar new year, and it also celebrates their spring. The North and South Vietnamese announced over the radio that there would be a cease-fire during the Tet holidays. War would stop for the celebration.

Dear Mom and Dad,

348 days left. Sounds like a lot, ha, well it is. I haven't had time to send the film home yet. I was sent out in the field Monday and got back in today. I didn't even take my writing paper out with me. The battalion has been out there for a month. We had to come in during the Vietnamese New Year because we're supposed to have some sort of peace agreement.

I hope that guy buys my car. I don't really want to mess with it when I get home.

I haven't written anyone yet but I didn't want to write until I got my address for sure then they sent me to the field and I forgot my stationary. I've got to start writing people but there are so many to write to I don't know where to start.

We have one good radio station here. It has my kind of music starting at 7 pm until? I never stayed up long enough to find out when it quits.

All these guys that sit around and talk about their R&R's get to you after a while. It seems like a long time until I get mine.

I'm going to close for now and see if I can write some more letters.

Love, Eddy

Chapter Fourteen
Tet

Vietnam
January 1968

The Viet Cong were scheming their infamous Tet offensive. The boy, like everyone he knew, was excited to be in on the plan to attack when everyone least expected it, during the Tet holiday on January 31st. He hated killing, and he knew this plan would end it all. They were going to overcome the Americans and get them out of his country, and they could be free of war at last. The plan for this immense operation took place in the underground tunnels around the American base of Cu Chi. This was his territory and he was in on something big, something that would end the war. His whole life, he'd only known oppression and war. He'd been a soldier for about eight years, since he was a boy, and he was still a survivor, unlike many of his loved ones and comrades. He was ready for this day when the war could end.

Chapter Fifteen
A Sinister Plot

Vietnam

January 1968

In the few days prior to Tet, Eddy and his platoon were in the field searching for enemy when ordered to return to base camp on the 28th of January. They looked forward to a break in the war due to the holiday. Eddy wrote this letter to my grandparents:

Dear Mom & Dad,

Well I got 4 letters written so far today.I wrote Mim, Lorine & Art, Gary & Jeanie, and Sandy. Now I'm writing you. This is a lot of writing, for me anyway.

We had today off more or less. I don't know why. I've been on patrols since 5 a.m. Saturday morning till 7 p.m. Sunday. We went on a company-sized ambush Saturday morning. We got in about 3:30 and had to get ready for a platoon-sized night ambush so I came in this morning about 7 and slept till noon. I went to the library this afternoon and wrote the 4 letters. I got tired of writing so went and took a shower, shaved and went to the PX. They didn't have any tooth brushes or mirrors there. That's what I went after.

Now I'm in the day room and I hope to get a few more letters written. We have a TV in here and there is some football game on. I don't know who is playing. I just got here.

Tomorrow is Tet. That's the Vietnamese New Year. Our EM club will be open again so things should be swinging.

I'm going to write Pastor and Mrs. Quebe. Maybe I won't. I forgot how to spell their name. Send me the address of the church and how their name is spelled.

Man, last night them damn mosquitoes almost ate me alive. I had my sleeves down and my collar buttoned up, but they got to my hands and face. Come to think of it that's something I forgot to buy at the PX, insect repellent.

I still haven't written David [his first cousin, who was also in Vietnam], but I'm going to write after I finish this letter. I'm carrying $60 with me still from my last paycheck. If I get quite a bit of money this paycheck I'll probably send most of it home. When I'm in the field I don't spend much money and that's where I'll be most of the time. That's good for saving money. We pay $5 a month for beer and soda. That assures us of getting one beer and one soda every night when we're in the field along with the hot meal we get. After eating C rations for breakfast and lunch that hot meal sure is good.

The football game that is playing is the Super Bowl. I heard part of it on the radio just after I got over here.

I should have gone swimming today, but then I wouldn't have gotten all these letters written. It's about chow time so I'm going to eat now.

Love, Eddy

P. S. Don't forget Pastor's address.
P. S. S. Thank you for the stationary, Dad, or writing tablet rather.

Although it was announced there would be no fighting during the Tet holiday, there was a sinister plot by the North Vietnamese to win the war by infiltrating and attacking cities and major command centers during the truce, when their enemy would be unprepared. It was a plan to take American troops by surprise. The Viet Cong sent more than 80,000 guerillas out of the jungles and tunnels to invade approximately a hundred cities and bases, while half of the American soldiers were on stand-down (not active—staying at base camp) due to the "truce." And so it was on that day, January 31st, 1968, the first day of Tet, that there were more American casualties than any other day of the war—245 American soldiers lost their lives in that one day. But Americans were not the only ones with losses; there were massive losses for the Viet Cong.

Chapter Sixteen
War Continues

Vietnam
February 1968

Like the rest of his comrades, the boy was disappointed. They thought the war was going to be over after January 31st. They had attacked several cities and major American bases, yet the Americans persisted and prevailed. Peace in his land seemed like a dream that would never come. Like the others, the boy was tired, but there was no such thing as being tired in his world, a world of violence, a world without freedom. His disappointment was deep, and he reached a point of thinking this war would never end, that he had been in war nearly his whole life, and war was going to continue until his life ended; that could be any day, any moment.

Chapter Seventeen
Search and Destroy

Vietnam
February 1968

During the Tet offensive, Eddy's platoon was sent to the field outside of Cu Chi as a reaction force, positioning for action that might occur. They were in a temporary overnight base camp called a logger site. A few days after Tet, on February 5th, their platoon departed on an "eagle flight" (a large air assault by helicopter), on a search and destroy mission. It was Eddy's first serious, intense battle against the Viet Cong. Early that morning several troops prepared to load into the utility helicopters known as Hueys (UH-1s). Eddy, Andy Wahrenbrock (the medic), Dave Glass, Larry Lundby (the newly married young man from Iowa), Jerry Miller and the two Texans, Jerry Counts and Robert Coulter crowded into one of them. "Hey Schultzie," Counts said to Eddy, once they were airborne, "get a look at those rice paddies." They were hanging on at the open door of the helicopter, and wind blew through like an instant air conditioner. They noted the rice paddies, the hedgerows and the lush, green jungle below but they felt pangs of fear when they remembered that in the midst of that beautiful land lurked the enemy in unseen places. The Huey transported them to a landing zone, which was a square area cleared of golden elephant grass that covered the ground like a thick shag carpet. The Hueys traveled in groups, landing like a flock of birds, onto the landing zone, in the midst of enemy territory. The knee-high grasses blew as if from an approaching tornado as the choppers hovered then set down as effortlessly as ducks landing on a lake. The chop-chop sound of the blades of several choppers was deafening. Eddy and the others jumped out of the Huey and scrambled into the jungle, trying to stay hidden, but, simultaneously staying alert for the enemy.

Throughout the jungle, the air was thick with humidity pressing into their lungs; with its unrelenting heaviness, it took its toll. In addition, Eddy was weighted down by his ammo belt, grenades, flairs, canteens, and miscellaneous other things. He carried his M-16 which weighed about nine pounds and the radio, a thirty pound square box, on his back. The antennae from the radio reached out above him like the antennae on a butterfly but he didn't feel like a butterfly, weighted down like he was. Those hot summer days baling hay paid off; he had the strength to do it. At around 1:00 p.m. they made contact with Viet Cong, and shots were fired back and forth. This was it, Eddy thought, the real thing. All of his training was for this moment. All of his life he played cowboys and Indians, cops and robbers, and now, this time, it was real. He and Andy stayed together, radio man and medic.

After a quick succession of wounded soldiers, most from other platoons, the officer in charge used Eddy's radio to call in a request for an airstrike and for a dust-off to collect the wounded. Their company pulled back to find cover, breaking contact with the enemy to allow jets to swoop in, drop bombs and napalm, killing and wounding unknown numbers of Viet Cong. Blasts of fire blazed through the trees, destroying all in its path and coming very close to their own troops. Eddy looked at his fellow soldiers, their faces and helmets black with soot and dirt, the whites of their eyes intensified from the contrast of their grimy, dark faces. After intense bombing, the jets took off, and Eddy's platoon, along with gunships, moved back in to continue their search for Viet Cong. They marched in a column. The lead person was called "point." To walk point took bravery, and it was nerve-wracking because they never knew what surprises lurked—Viet Cong, booby-traps, tigers—and the man in lead was sure to get it first if he wasn't careful. Often Dave was the one to walk point. They had to whack their way through the jungle areas with machetes. It wasn't long before they encountered more enemy and their column had to spread out so they wouldn't shoot the guy in front of them. In the firefight, bullets hit three feet away from Eddy and Andy. One of their guys was hit in the neck. Andy, who was the medic, opened his first aid bag, cleaned the wound, bandaged him and announced that it wasn't deep, that he got lucky and was only scraped by the bullet; he would be okay. But others weren't so lucky. By the end of the day, four men were killed and seven wounded from their company, Charlie Company. At 5:30 p.m., after six hours of intense combat, they broke from the enemy and were airlifted out. It was a day of hell on earth. Eddy managed to write two letters, with no mention of the battle he had just experienced. The first was dated February 6th and the second, February 8th. Here are excerpts:

Dear Mom and Dad,

> *Sorry I haven't written sooner but I've been quite busy lately. How is everything back home? I guess Pacho [Sandy's dog] is doing fine.*
>
> *What is the story on the pictures, my car and the sheep? I hope those pictures have come in. If you get this letter before you send that picture to Mim, use some of my money and buy a nice picture frame for it; if you have already sent it, forget the frame. It was just a thought in case you hadn't sent it.*
>
> *Now has that kid said any more about buying my car? You can do what you want with the stereo.*
>
> *Are the sheep all doing fine? And have any been sold? If you two need any money to get something you want or any emergencies don't be afraid to use the money in my savings. Your credit is good anytime with me. If Dad needs any of the money for farming or livestock use it for that. It's a good investment.*
>
> *The mail here has been messed up so if you don't hear from me for a long time it's the mail system. Our post office burned up so I don't know what was in there. That didn't speed up anything.*
>
> *Tell everybody hi. In the field I can't write letters to anyone except you and Mim. Those are the only addresses I've memorized. "Happy Valentine's day".   Love, Eddy*

Dear Mom and Dad,

We haven't done too much for the last couple of days. We did change logger sites so this way we don't eagle flight out every day; we're close enough to walk now.

There was something I forgot to ask in the last letter and I can't think of what it was now.

I'm hoping we'll be able to go back to Dau Tieng in 3 or 4 days. I've been wearing and working in the same clothes for a week and a half. We can wash up with our steel pots [helmets] but then you put the same clothes on again.

I remember what I forgot. What happened to that bond election ballot? And what time do I write in for the presidential ballot?

We have a paper published in Vietnam called Stars and Stripes. It keeps us informed on what's happening back in the world. Believe it or not I read most of it, mainly cause there's nothing else to do.

Today I have one month in country, just 11 more to go and if I get a Christmas drop it's only 10 more. Monsoon season will be here in a couple of months and things really cool off then, not just the sun either, I mean the war.

I think I told you I'm an R.T.O. (radio telephone operator) now. I carry a radio on my back. That radio gets pretty heavy after 4,000 meters. It's a pretty good job though and I'll get used to carrying it.

I need a haircut pretty bad now. The last time we were in base camp the barber shop was closed because of Tet.

If you have time send me some cookies and

that stuff you make instant pudding with—the
chocolate. I can fix stuff like that in base camp.
I guess I'll be going now.

Love, Eddy

On the day he wrote this letter, his platoon was ordered to take the village of Tan Hoa.

Chapter Eighteen
Tan Hoa

Vietnam
February 1968

The village of Tan Hoa was near Cu Chi, the base where Eddy spent his first five days "in-country" and close to the logger sites where they had spent the previous few days. Cu Chi was a major American base, headquarters to the 25th infantry division (of which Eddy was a part of), and because of this, Viet Cong invaded nearby Tan Hoa to interrupt the convoy of American goods on the supply road between Cu Chi and Saigon. The inhabitants and civilians of Tan Hoa fled in fear, disappearing into the thick jungle where monkeys wailed and tigers lurked, and also into neighboring villages. Eddy's entire battalion, not just his platoon, was ordered to take the village of Tan Hoa. As his platoon arrived, they witnessed the last of the villagers fleeing with their water buffalo. First in was D Company, then C Company (Eddy's). A and B Companies were dropped in by helicopter for support. The Viet Cong were prepared for battle and well-armed with fifty-one caliber machine guns and rocket launchers. They had built concrete bunkers throughout the village. Their underground tunnel system allowed them to be everywhere and nowhere. They acted with stealth, and were as quiet as the soft footsteps of a tiger on a jungle hunt the moment before its prey was pounced. They fought hard, and would disappear underground only to pop out of the ground again several yards away. American troops never knew where to aim. A Viet Cong woman in a spider hole kept popping up with a machine gun, firing everywhere, then retreating into the hole like a vermin, only to suddenly pop up again, firing vehemently. This went on all day, until a G. I. finally stopped her with a hand grenade. She was only one of many women Viet Cong soldiers and snipers. It was Feb. 8th, 1968. It was over a hundred degrees with high humidity, and Jerry Counts had only three canteens of water. He ran out by noon, as did most of the others. This happened every day. They called for more supplies but wouldn't get them until a day later. They were on their bellies for most of the fighting. It was a tough battle which didn't end on the first day or the second day; it raged on for six days. It was the worst fighting some of Eddy's platoon had ever seen. Finally on Feb. 14th, Valentine's Day, they "cleaned out" the village and were able to walk through, having killed 122 Viet Cong, though they lost about 45 from their own battalion. They were commended by the commander for taking on a much greater force than they were, and coming out ahead. One Vietnam vet told me the one thing that was harder than killing others, was the praise they received for doing so.

The Viet Cong had seventy-five miles (121 km) of underground tunnels surrounding the area of Cu Chi, which connected to thousands of miles of tunnels that meandered throughout their country. The Viet Cong guerilla fighters and the North Vietnamese Army (NVA) soldiers popped up out of the ground at any moment, or disappeared into what seemed like thin air. The tunnels had three levels including barracks for sleeping and hospitals to care for their injured. It was a world underground. American soldiers were above ground and Viet Cong soldiers were underneath them, showing up at random moments. Eddy and his fellow soldiers were in constant danger of Viet Cong and of booby traps. They were warned to never pick up beer cans, canteens or any item they saw on the ground or anywhere because a grenade could be tied to it or inside of it. Eleven percent of American soldiers in Vietnam were killed by booby traps.

One day Jerry Counts and Robert Coulter, the two Texans, saw an abandoned motorcycle along the side of a dirt road. Robert said, "Let's ride it!"

Jerry said, "It could be booby-trapped!"

Later they saw it still there. Robert said, "Get it Counts!"

Jerry said, "Booby trap!" But the temptation was greater than their fear. They inched toward it. They searched around for a sign of life lurking behind trees and saw no one. They debated back and forth whether or not to touch the thing. Finally, temptation won and they risked it, hopped on and, since it didn't explode, they raced it around, finally abandoning it in a nearby village.

On Feb. 23rd, which was my mom and dad's 22nd wedding anniversary, Eddy's platoon went on a mission to sweep and patrol a different village. Mechanized infantry tanks and trucks moved in to support them. Armored personnel carriers (APCs) were called "battle taxis" or "battle busses" by the troops. The M113, the most common APC, was on tracks rather than wheels. A fifty caliber machine gun was mounted to the top and there were sixteen soldiers inside. The carrier's main purpose was for transporting troops, not for combat. But on this morning the APC was caught in the midst of an explosive fire power exchange. The driver of the APC, in haste to pull back from the Viet Cong, put it in reverse. Since there was chaos all around, and there were troops behind the APC, it backed over two American soldiers, killing one, wounding the other. Later, again in haste to pull back, it backed over another of their own, a young, blonde draftee. It knocked him down, rolled over him, and crushed him to death. For Eddy and some of the others, this was their first brutal experience of seeing their own men killed by their own men. He'd heard stories of soldiers getting killed by "friendly fire," by their own weapons, but to actually be there when it happened was another thing. So many dangers lurked—the jungle was booby trapped by VC, there were leeches, red ants, tigers, the VC popped out of the ground any time, any place, and to add to that the dangers within their own was unfathomable. I'm certain Eddy thought of these boys' families finding out that their sons were killed, and by their own company. He knew, but for the grace of God, it could have been him.

Despite these casualties, they made contact with the enemy several times on this mission. At one point, the Viet Cong shot at least ten rounds hitting too close between Andy and Eddy. They backed out of the village twice, but kept returning in until nightfall, three times in before they returned to base camp. They all thought about survival. They'd made it through one more day, one more battle where not everyone was as lucky. The next day, on Feb. 24th, Eddy wrote home, with no mention of the dangers:

Dear Mom and Dad,

I have been getting quite a few letters lately, but at the first of the month I hardly got anything, our mail was pretty screwed up then. You mentioned something about a long letter 5 pages, well I never got it. I did get Karen's letter and a couple letters from Lynne. She also said she sent some cookies, but it takes a while to get packages here so I hope to get hers and the one you sent. I just got your package and ate half the nuts, one can of peaches and I can hardly wait to try the shake-a-pudding. I'm eating the applesauce right now. It's all good. Thank you very much. We've been in the field for 24 days now and we don't get many treats so the package came at a really good time.

I'm fine here and when most of the fighting broke out I was in Dau Tieng; it didn't get hit so no problem there [probably referring to the TET offensive which was all over the news]. Right now I'm in a fire support base camp just outside of Saigon.

Well I fixed one pudding up. It's setting now so in a few minutes I will let you know how it is.

We should be going back into Dau Tieng in a few days at least before pay day. The $170 I sent was sent the same time as the $100 I sent before, *through the government, so it should get there or be there by now.*

The sun gets awful hot in the afternoon but it cools off real nice in the evening; gets kind of cold in early mornings though.

Well that pudding is great. You might have gotten yourself into something now. I'll have you send that stuff more often. It's perfect when you're out in the boonies like this. I've got a lot of help eating it too.

Oh yeah, thanks for the color film. I'm going to start bringing my camera out in the field. We have a lot of pretty country around here.

I haven't had time to send the used film yet or my W-2 form since I haven't been in base camp. I'll send it as soon as possible.

It's impossible to stay clean out here. We have no showers and the dust is thick. It sure will be nice to get back to base camp, take a shower and put on clean clothes. If I forget to tell you anything just let me know. I'll write when I can.

Love, Eddy

Grandma always sent Eddy food, so he shared it. That's the way it was in Vietnam. If somebody had something, they shared with the others. They were family; each other was all they had. Grandma sent a white cake. Eddy cut it into twelve slices with his utility knife. Jerry reached out for that cake and noticed the contrast between his filthy hand, black from dirt and sweat, and that white slice of sweetness. He said to Eddy, "Schultzie, thank your mama for me!" Eddy wrote this letter to his parents on Feb. 28th:

Dear Mom and Dad & Sandy,

> *We got to stay back today so I have time to write. I got a letter from David [his cousin] and finally wrote him a letter last night.*
> *I lost all my sleeping gear and writing paper plus what was left of the pudding and that color film, boy did that make me mad. We put our sleeping gear, and excess equipment in B bags (blanket bags) because it's too much to carry while we're in the field. We move around a lot and somehow they lost the B bag my stuff was in. It's the second or third time they lost one of our bags. Sleeping gear we can turn in to Combat-Lost and get new stuff but anything not army issue we're out of luck.*
> *The mail system here is really messed up. I don't know how it is back in the states.*
> *This is all the stationary I could find today so this won't be a long letter.*
> *How is everyone at home? Is Sandy still going to be leaving for Germany the first week in March? I haven't written Sal yet, but then his address was with the stuff I lost.*

Lots of Love, Eddy

Chapter Nineteen
Hoc Mon

Vietnam
March 1968

On the second of March, two days before a major battle that Eddy was in, he wrote this letter to my family. There were others he wrote to us, but they are missing. This is the only one we have. However, most of his letters were to Grandma, Grandpa and Maryanne.

Dear Lorine, Art and Family,

I've been getting quite a few letters from your family and haven't had time to write back. I lost all my stationary which didn't help matters any. I've been out in the field since the 1st of February and it doesn't look like we'll be going back to base camp for quite a while. It's hard to get stationary out here so I'm just writing one letter to the whole family.

We're looking for the rockets they've been firing at Tan san Nhut Air Base and we don't go back to base camp until we find them. Our base camp has been getting mortared three times a day so we're probably better off out in the field.

I still haven't gotten the cookies Lynne sent, but the mail gets messed up sometimes so they should be getting here pretty soon.

We get in a little action now and then, but things have cooled down quite a bit since the 1st so it's not so bad anymore.

We get one hot meal a day, a goody pack (candy) and a soda and beer every night. And no place to spend money so I've been sending $170 home. I give $5 for the beer and soda for a month. I keep what's left, about $14. When I go into Dau Tieng again that gives me something to spend at the P.X. Since swimming is free and so are movies if they ever have any. Then there's always the E.M. Club of course, but beer is only 15¢ a can.

Some of the guys just fixed up some good ol' sweet corn. We picked it out in a field right outside of our perimeter. Man was it good.

Our medic is going into one of the base camps tonight with some guy who just went crazy, so I'm having him pick up some writing paper for me.

I better go for now. Good luck in school Lynne, Judy, Arthur and Karen.

Love, Eddy

On March 4th, 1968, like every other morning at that time of year out in the field, when Eddy woke after sleeping on the ground in his "poncho liner" (a blanket that his head fits through so that the blanket surrounds him) there was a slight chill to the air yet the humidity was already threatening. On this morning, they were ordered into the northeast side of Hoc Mon District, near the tiny village of Hoc Mon, in the Gia Dinh Province, on a search and destroy mission. The Viet Cong were launching rockets into Tan san Nhut Air Base, and Eddy's platoon was sent in to stop the attack. They were to approach the area from one side while another company approached from the other side, hoping to push the Viet Cong one direction or the other. His platoon loaded into the Huey that would fly them to this area north of Saigon, though the group of young soldiers had no idea of the names of the tiny villages. Two days before getting onto the chopper, one of the men panicked. He had a dream that they were all going to die. He fell apart, screaming, panicking, so Pappy Steele, their sergeant, ordered Andy, the medic, to return him to base camp. Andy led the man to base camp and knew it meant his platoon would be going without him. Another medic, Doc Lasister, would be going. So when the chopper took off, Andy wasn't on it with the rest of his platoon. I'm sure it felt weird to Eddy to not have Andy by his side. They'd been together constantly. When the chopper landed after a short flight, they jumped into the deafening sound of rotor blades. The wind from the whirring blades pushed against them as if to warn them and propel them back into the safety of the helicopter. Carrying their rifles and loaded down with about seventy pounds of equipment on their backs and bodies, the moment they set foot upon ground, they ran from the helicopter clearing toward the thick jungle, and formed their column with point man up front. They eventually came to rice fields, which, from the air had looked like a patchwork quilt, with large squares of planted land and each plot completely bordered by hedgerows. Eddy had made it through a few battles now, and this would be one more he had to face, with nine more months ahead of him and countless more battles.

Chapter Twenty
The Boy's Village

Vietnam
March 1968

The boy's village of Hoc Mon was no longer home. It was abandoned by the villagers, his family and friends, and was now in the middle of a war zone. He was with his comrades, ordered to be in his very own village, hiding in the abandoned huts where he grew up, waiting for the American soldiers to move in closer. Their soldiers were not quiet like they thought they were. Like his comrades, he probably had thoughts like these: We always knew where they were. They had loud voices and left beer cans, soda cans and other trash wherever they went. They smoked cigarettes and played music. They stomped through our jungles and made paths for themselves, chopping down trees and vines. He wondered about them, and about how abrasive and loud they could be. He could hear them laugh sometimes too, and yell. They were so different. They seemed so naïve and open, like an open book that wouldn't close. The boy and his comrades learned to be silent, swift and quick. The American voices rang out, and though the boy hated them because they were the enemy and invading his land, he also felt in awe of who they seemed to be, those voices that echoed through the jungle with the mixture of courage and innocence.

He could hear them coming. And so, the boy sat in his ruined home, and waited. Fear had left his body years before. There was nothing for him but war, waiting, and the constant thought of death, which was attached to him like a shadow. Yet he kept surviving. He could hear the enemy. They did not understand silence. They were getting close.

Chapter Twenty-One
Two Worlds Collide

Vietnam
March 1968

Pappy Steele always gave sound, well-respected orders to his troops. But there was another sergeant walking point that day in the Hoc Mon area. He was up front, pushing fast, pushing everyone to surge ahead. He was a gung-ho type of guy, who often barked orders and acted before he thought things through. Dave Glass, the sergeant from Minnesota, was toward the back, and at first couldn't see what was happening up front. He hollered, "We're moving too fast! We're not checking hooches!" He felt they weren't ready for defensive action. But the troops followed behind the anxious sergeant who urged them forward, who rushed in like a horse with blinders on. Before long, their platoon along with other platoons in their company were scattered and not in the column as they should have been. Eddy's job as RTO (radio man) was to stay near Pappy Steele, their sergeant. Eddy and Pappy were behind Larry Lundby and Jerry Counts, who were ahead of the rest of the platoon, following behind the gung-ho sergeant. They headed toward the abandoned village of Hoc Mon (*where the boy listened and waited*), where they had hoped to hide out as they targeted the Viet Cong whom they knew were nearby.

The platoon moved quickly through the rice fields compared to how slow and tedious it was to clear a path with machetes through the thickly jungled terrain. As they approached the village, they were taken by surprise, ambushed, when the Viet Cong, who were already in the village, hiding in the abandoned huts and large bunkers, sprayed them with a barrage of bullets, without letup, like a sudden thunderstorm. With instinctual reactions, Eddy's platoon dropped onto their bellies, returning fire from ground level. There were more Viet Cong than they had anticipated and the constant stream of bullets bombarded them, striking everywhere. Their eager sergeant who was up front was hit in the back. Despite bullets flying all around him, Doc Lasister raced toward the sergeant, bandaged him and stayed with him, leading him away from the front line to be medevacked out in the first dust-off. The infantry medics were the bravest of men, as they had to rush into the line of fire to help the wounded. Eddy was still near the front with Pappy but behind "Lumpy," Larry Lundby, who was up front near the hit sergeant. Jerry Counts was near the front too, carrying a sixty caliber machine gun. Lundby, who was Jerry's close friend, motioned for Jerry to bring the machine gun up front. Bullets flew and struck all around them. Jerry scrambled on the ground toward Lundby, who quickly started feeding the machine gun. It jammed. With adrenalin scrambling through their veins, they managed to unjam it, as bullets rained around them. Jerry fired back, about 400 rounds, when the gun jammed again. Lundby barely raised his chest off the ground, but enough to take a bullet straight through his heart. Jerry witnessed his friend die immediately; he felt like he was in the midst of a nightmare. Through the noise of raining bullets, he heard Pappy holler to him, "Counts, get over here. I've got ammo for you!" Though in shock over losing his buddy, he followed the order and scrambled toward Pappy, but everything seemed surreal and in slow motion. Pappy and Eddy were on their bellies, shooting, when Jerry raced toward them for more ammo.

Dave was still in the rear, but he had moved up enough that he could now see what was going on. When he saw their sergeant and Lundby get hit, he hollered, "I'm coming up!"

"No!" shouted Pappy. "Stay where you're at. Find cover!"

The platoon began a slow retreat, scooting backwards on their bellies, still shooting at the enemy, reaching the hedgerow at the same time that Jerry reached Eddy and Pappy. They felt they were in the midst of hell.

Chapter Twenty-Two
The Telegram

San Luis Obispo, California
March 1968

Usually I'm a sound sleeper and will sleep through alarm clocks and phones ringing, but this night, I can't sleep. I feel jittery, like popcorn. I get a horrible pain in my leg, and I let out a scream because it hurts a lot and I don't know what it is. Mom rushes in and announces that I have a charlie horse. She explains it's a muscle cramp and to stretch my foot back and forth. It starts to dissipate, but I still can't sleep. I feel uneasy and nervous as if I have to do an oral presentation at school tomorrow but I don't.

In the morning, on March 9th, 1968 my friend, Shelley, picks me up to carpool to our classes at Cuesta College. For some reason I feel uneasy all day and Shelley isn't at our meeting place when it's time to go home. We had been carpooling since September and she had never forgotten me before, which adds to my strange feeling. I call home, thinking someone might be home to come get me. Dad answers. I wonder why he's home from work in the middle of the day. He says he'll come get me. Instead, in twenty minutes I see Shelley pull up.

"Why are you picking me up and not my dad?" I say, after asking why she forgot me.

"He called and asked me to."

"But why wouldn't he come?" That isn't like Dad. He always drives us kids around to the store, to friends' houses, wherever, whenever we need a ride. "And why is he even home?"

But Shelley doesn't answer. My uneasy feeling grows in intensity. My dad sells insurance and has a fairly flexible schedule, but still, he usually wasn't home mid-afternoon. I feel the same as I did all night, like popcorn was inside trying to burst free. I bombard Shelley with questions. "What did he say? Did he tell you why he was home? Why didn't he come get me?"

Shelley says nothing except that she doesn't know. By the time I'm home I'm almost hysterical. I burst through the door, hollering to anyone, "What is going on?"

I realize everyone is there—Dad, Judy, Arthur, and Mom, who is home from work and it's only 3:00. "What? What? What?" I shriek, louder with each word. Judy and Arthur are on the couch, looking like zombies and they don't answer. They are dazed, expressionless, adding to my fears.

Dad says, "Come here." He takes me into Karen's room and for a second looks at her bed while trying to form his words.

"Karen?" I cry in a high pitched voice. I'm suddenly realizing she's the only one not home. She's only five, and just the other day she had to go to the doctor for bruises on her legs, which we thought might be leukemia.

"No, Karen is fine," he quickly says. Then, it's so hard for him, but his words tumble out and it's like a slow motion movie, when he says, "It's Eddy."

"No!" I scream it like I'm pierced with a knife, knowing he's in a war, knowing the danger. "No!!! No!!!" I feel my chest cave in. I feel this is not real, not happening. "No!"

Dad quickly adds, "He's missing. They haven't found him. He's missing in action. Grandma and Grandpa were told this morning." The piercing slightly lets up and I feel there is hope. He has to be alive, I think. He has to be.

I'm in shock and scared. Mom is sobbing in the back room. Judy and Arthur start crying too and so do I. All night, all day, I'd been anxious and didn't know why. My subconscious must have known—a premonition. I can't imagine what Grandma and Grandpa are going through. Grandpa has been working diligently restoring that Mercedes for Eddy. The grief is going to kill him. Dad has his arms wrapped around Mom and they are both crying. Dad had been dating Mom for three years when her baby brother was born four months before they were married, so he knew Eddy as well as she did. I'd only seen Dad cry once before, when his father died. He'd watched this little boy grow up, for twenty-one years. Karen's babysitter, who lives at the corner, brings her home since none of us are up to walking the three doors down to get her. Karen learns that Eddy is missing and she watches all of us in our grief; she's tells us all that he'll be found.

That morning, my grandparents received the following telegram:

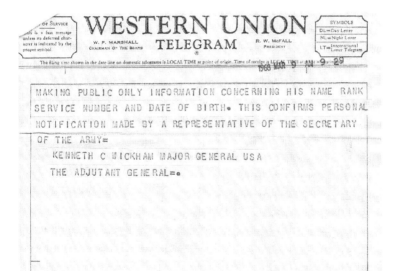

WESTERN UNION
TELEGRAM

CLASS OF SERVICE
This is a fast message unless its deferred character is indicated by the proper symbol.

W. P. MARSHALL
CHAIRMAN OF THE BOARD

R. W. McFALL
PRESIDENT

SYMBOLS
DL = Day Letter
NL = Night Letter
LT = International Letter Telegram

The filing time shown in the date line on domestic telegrams is LOCAL TIME at point of origin. Time of receipt is LOCAL TIME at point of destination

1968 MAR 8 PM 29

LB005 SPD061 PA054 =

L P WB018 XV TOVT PDB=FAX WASHINGTON DC 9=

MR AND MRS SAMUEL C SCHULTZ DONT PHONE DONT DELV BTWN

10PM AND 6AM= 1344 CECILIA COURT SANLUIS OBISPO CALIF=

=THE SECRETARY OF THE ARMY HAS ASKED ME TO EXPRESS HIS
DEEP REGRET THAT YOUR SON PRIVATE FIRST CLASS EDWARD A
SCHULTZ HAS BEEN MISSING VIETNAM SINCE 4 MARCH 1968. HE
WAS LAST SEEN ON A COMBAT OPERATION WHEN ENGAGED A HOSTILE
FORCE IN A FIREFIGHT. SEARCH IS IN PROGRESS. YOU WILL BE
ADVISED PROMPTLY WHEN FURTHER INFORMATION IS RECEIVED. IN
ORDER TO PROTECT ANY INFORMATION THAT MIGHT BE USED TO
YOUR SONS DETRIMENT YOUR COOPERATION IS REQUESTED IN

WU1201 (R2-65)   THE COMPANY WILL APPRECIATE SUGGESTIONS FROM ITS PATRONS CONCERNING ITS SERVICE

WESTERN UNION
TELEGRAM

OF SERVICE
This is a fast message unless its deferred character is indicated by the proper symbol.

W. P. MARSHALL
CHAIRMAN OF THE BOARD

R. W. McFALL
PRESIDENT

SYMBOLS
DL = Day Letter
NL = Night Letter
LT = International Letter Telegram

The filing time shown in the date line on domestic telegrams is LOCAL TIME at point of origin. Time of receipt is LOCAL TIME at point of destination

1968 MAR 8 PM 29

MAKING PUBLIC ONLY INFORMATION CONCERNING HIS NAME RANK
SERVICE NUMBER AND DATE OF BIRTH. THIS CONFIRMS PERSONAL
NOTIFICATION MADE BY A REPRESENTATIVE OF THE SECRETARY
OF THE ARMY=
KENNETH C WICKHAM MAJOR GENERAL USA
THE ADJUTANT GENERAL=.

WU1201 (R2-65)   THE COMPANY WILL APPRECIATE SUGGESTIONS FROM ITS PATRONS CONCERNING ITS SERVICE

A week later we are told Eddy is dead. I remember being told that he was found in a hospital and that his entire platoon had been killed in a mine explosion and that his body had been missing from theirs because he'd been transported to the hospital. Our worst fear realized. My whole family can't stop crying. I'm sick in my stomach and can't believe Eddy is dead, gone, never to be seen again. He won't return to us. He won't teach Karen how to ride Cayenne. He won't drive that Mercedes. He won't become the ranch manager he dreamed of. He won't marry Maryanne and have children. He won't flash that heart-warming smile at any of us again. He's gone, in a foreign land, with no family at his side. He's gone, and I think how nobody over there remembers him because his whole platoon is gone too. Like he fell into a black hole.

Mom and Dad won't allow me to see the viewing of his body. They come home from it, devastated. I'm angry they went without me. I desperately want to see him one last time. I need to say good-bye. They're adamant and won't let me go. I'm enraged. I argue, I yell at them, I cry. I'm eighteen and know I can get in the car and go by myself, and I thought of doing so, but at a deeper level, I know they're wise and they wouldn't argue this much without good reason. Judy is smart enough to not want to go, but she sees me arguing with them and wonders why I'm making a big deal of it. She wants to remember him as he was. I finally accept that it's for my best interest and I quit arguing. Sandy, who is twenty-three and did go, says that I'm lucky I didn't go. She says, "Be glad you have no memory of what I saw. Remember all the years with him and the last time you saw him because if you'd seen what I saw it's hard to get it from your mind." Perhaps her words are the reason I etch the memories of Eddy in my brain. I think about everything I can remember. I keep hearing his words, his voice and seeing the moments in time with Eddy over and over again so I will never forget him. I love my parents more than ever for saving me from the additional pain they and Sandy feel by viewing his body.

Judy comes home from school one day before the funeral and tells us she was looking out the window while in class, in deep shock, unable to believe this devastating loss. Her teacher says, "Miss Ludwick, are you paying attention here?" It was just any other day to the teacher. She looks at the teacher but can't say, "No, I'm not. I just lost my uncle in the war!!!" She can't say it, so she sits in silence, mourning, still unable to pay attention.

I can't fathom that he's dead. It's like a tree yanked from my heart, leaving a gaping dark void. Our entire family is devastated. He was the baby to his four siblings and parents. He was revered and the trail blazer to his string of nieces and nephews.

The funeral is at the Zion Lutheran Church on March 21st, 1968 at 1:00 p.m. Sitting in the family section I can't stop my tears. I'm in my own cocoon of pain, as is the rest of my family. Six of his young friends, including his best friend, Tom St. John, are casket bearers. The eulogy is given by Pastor Stanley Quebe, who knew him since he was a boy of five, a boy who felt at home at Sunday school and church, who spent every Sunday there for most of his life. The words sprang from the pastor's heart, and from sixteen years of knowing this child who was barely grown:

Edward was a young man who wanted peace just as God wanted him to have it. He was a farmer who wanted his tractor, not tanks; he wanted his plow, not a rifle. But he went when he was called. He didn't want war but he did what he thought was right for his country. Now he has the peace God has promised for all of us.

Our family is sitting together in a private area where we couldn't see the crowd. When I stand to leave, I'm shocked to see how the church is packed with people filling the spaces along the back and side aisles. When we go outside to climb into the limo, we see people who had been unable to get in crowded at the front door. Police arrive to direct traffic. We ride to the cemetery in the limo and I see that both Santa Rosa Street and Foothill Boulevard are lined with parked cars. High school friends, college friends, church friends, neighbors, family, wrestling friends, FFA friends, track team friends all come to mourn. At the cemetery, we sit in the front row, and I see a sea of people surrounding the seated area, so many people, so many faces. Through my tears, I see a familiar face in the front line of the crowd. He was in Eddy's class, and is a friend of mine. He winks at me, I feel his compassion, and I realize how every small amount of support feels like a foundation to steady yourself upon.

I can't help tears, and wish they would stop. I'm not good at hiding my feelings. My grandmother is holding back tears and I wonder how she can do it. Maybe years of experience, years of loss have given her the strength to get through this day when she buries the second of her six children, her youngest child, her baby, the boy we all loved.

Chapter Twenty-Three
Forty Years Later
California
2008

It had been a lie. He was never missing in action like the telegram said. And somehow Judy and I had been told he was found in a hospital and that his entire platoon had been killed. This wasn't true either, but we didn't know that until forty years later. My brother only remembers that there were two different stories about his death, like we'd been told one thing and then another, but he doesn't remember the details of either version. Sandy remembers the correct facts, but agrees that we were told he was missing in action.

Andy Wahrenbrock, the medic, and Jerry Counts, one of the boys from Texas, knew the true story of Eddy's death because they were there, they saw it with their own eyes, they were in his platoon, they were his "brothers," his platoon family and they did not die, like I had always thought. A few months after Eddy was killed, Andy was hit by friendly fire, a mortar from our own planes hit him in the hip. He returned home after having been in Vietnam six months. But that six months caused a lifetime of pain, emotional and physical.

Andy couldn't talk about the war for many years; it opened wounds too deep. But twenty-five years later the thoughts began to creep in. He eventually tried to make contact with our family. He called Grandma, who was in her mid-eighties. He explained he had been friends with Eddy in Vietnam. He said she didn't have questions, didn't say much, and he felt like it was a dead end. He wanted to communicate what he knew, to meet the family. But Grandma, a reserved and quiet woman, rarely talked of her suffering, and this loss, her second loss of a child, and though she felt it very deeply, was no exception. I remember her telling me that someone had called her, someone who had been with Eddy in Vietnam, but she didn't say anything else about it.

Thank goodness for the Internet because that's how Andy found us, the rest of Eddy's family. Ten years passed after his contact with Grandma, when my sister, Judy, posted a remembrance of Eddy on the Vietnam Veteran's Memorial website. Andy saw it and wrote to her at once.

I got a call from Judy. "There's a fellow who's going to send you an email about Eddy," she said. In corresponding with Andy it was decided that he would drive from Bakersfield to my house in Atascadero to meet the family and to share what he knew of Eddy's time in Vietnam. I invited relatives and made a lot of food. Sandy and Sal, my uncle Gary and his wife, Jeanie, my mother, Lorine, and her new husband, Guy (my father had died in 1985 after thirty-nine years of marriage), Judy, and Eddy's high school friend, Tom St. John. Karen lived too far away and Arthur was out of town. My cousin, John, and his wife drove from San Jose. Grandma died on January 3, 2002, just shy of turning ninety-six, so she wasn't at this event.

Andy Wahrenbrock is a gentle, quiet, reflective man. He brought pictures, articles, a map of Vietnam and his diary entry from March third and fourth. He spoke in a steady, somber tone, "When Eddy arrived, I had only been there a short time. We were both from California and we hit it off immediately. He was the radio man and I was the medic so we were required to stay together at all times. We were out in the field most of the days he was there."

What Andy told us opened long buried wounds, but in the way a doctor might have to break a bone to reset it properly, this was necessary for us to heal properly. He shared with us how, about a month after the Tet offensive, their platoon headed into the deserted village in the Hoc Mon area on a mission to look for Viet Cong who had been launching rockets into the Tan san Nhut Air Base near Saigon. He put me in contact with Jerry Counts, from Texas, who shared more of Eddy's death. This is the true story of how Eddy died on March 4th, 1968, and the remainder of the story of his last battle, so far from home near the tiny village called Hoc Mon:

"Counts, bring the machine gun over here and I'll load it for you," Pappy hollered above the deafening sounds of major fire power. Jerry scrambled toward Pappy, though in shock over losing his best friend, Larry Lundby; everything seemed surreal. He scooted along the hedgerow toward Eddy and Pappy, who, like everyone else, were on their bellies, on the ground, with rifles aimed at the enemy. Pappy had the ammunition Jerry needed, but Pappy was on the other side of Eddy. Jerry crawled over Eddy to get to Pappy, crouching as low as he could and as close over Eddy as he could, to avoid the bombarding bullets. Eddy had the radio on his back, so it put Jerry a little higher than he wanted to be. The exact moment he was above Eddy a bullet struck Eddy in the head. Jerry fell onto the ground next to Eddy. It was a scene imprinted in his brain forever. Wade Lasister was the medic who quickly worked on Eddy, but there was nothing he could do. In an instant, the life was gone out of the little boy who cheered, "We want a touchdown," who dreamt of managing a ranch, who earned the State Farmer award, who was engaged to marry Maryanne, who was the nicest boy anyone could know. For Jerry, it was a nightmare. First Lundby then Eddy, whom he called, "Schultzie." He had watched two friends die gruesome deaths right before his eyes in a matter of moments. Finally, the third platoon relieved them so they could take out their four wounded and two dead. Jerry's tears streamed down his dirty face, as he pulled Eddy and Larry's lifeless, heavy bodies toward the medivac, or "dust-off" chopper. Eddy's short life of twenty-one years ended that day in Hoc Mon, Gia Dinh Province, Vietnam, doing, without complaint, what he was told to do by his government, but it was the last thing his heart, his farmer's heart, had wanted to do.

When the dust-off arrived at base camp, Andy, feeling distraught because he'd heard the firefight over his radio, was the first to greet the helicopter and identify Eddy and Larry. Andy felt distressed because he wasn't there with his fellow troops due to being sent back with the soldier who had the breakdown. To discover that his best friend, Eddy, and his other friend, Larry, had both been killed was devastating. This was a moment that would haunt him his whole life.

Eddy's platoon backed out for a short time, while they got their wounded and two dead into dust-offs, but they went back in later that evening, and they fought through two or three days until they cleaned out the village and won the battle.

What we had believed for forty years, what the government had told us, was not true. He had never been missing in action. I asked Andy why the government would make up things that weren't true. He said the best that he could figure is that they just didn't know. It was a chaotic time, and the facts were not always known by those in charge.

Judy and I had believed that all of Eddy's platoon had died, and that Eddy had been found in a hospital where he died. It turns out that Sandy, and Uncle Gary don't remember this. They were told he died in a firefight, which is what happened. In looking through papers, I found the letter to my grandparents from the government that confirms he died in a firefight, which is also confirmed by the eye witness account of Jerry Counts, who was next to him when he died, and of Andy Wahrenbrock, who was first to see and identify his body when the dust-off arrived to base camp. I guess we will never know why Judy and I had believed something different for so many years, but I feel relieved to learn that the rest of Eddy's platoon didn't die that day. The fact that they've been meeting every year since the year 2000 and remembering Eddy and Larry, the two they lost on March 4th, 1968 makes it less dark, less like he had fallen into a deep dark abyss as if nobody knew he'd been there or existed. These men knew him, fought beside him and remembered him. I'm forever grateful to Andy Wahrenbrock for reaching out to our family.

Andy Wahrenbrock visits my family; 2008.

Sandy and Andy.

Members of Eddy's platoon visit with my daughter, Lauren, and me, in New Mexico; 2012.

Me and Lauren; trip home from the platoon reunion.

Chapter Twenty-Four
The War Ends

Vietnam

March 1968–April 1975

The boy who had only known war his whole life was a survivor again, despite American soldiers eventually winning this battle in his home village of Hoc Mon. He lost many comrades that day, and he fought in and survived many battles after that.

The American military pulled out of Vietnam five years later, in August of 1973, but the war between north and south continued. Twenty months later, the war came to a close on April 30th, 1975 when the North Vietnamese Army captured Saigon. The boy lived through it all, and lived to see his dream, the reunification of North and South Vietnam. His prized possession was the battle flag which had seen him through every battle, and had proudly flown at most of them. To him, the flag represented the courage of the Viet Cong, the sacrifices, the losses, and it also represented their honor and their success in achieving the goal of unification.

The devastation and loss was great. It's estimated that approximately a million Vietnamese lost their lives in this war. The boy had lost many loved ones and friends, including the elderly, women, and children. He wondered about his fate, and why he had been chosen to survive through all those years of war and destruction.

Chapter Twenty-Five
The Box

California
2010

I hold the tarnished metal box and before I open it, I think of how it came to be in my hands, and the violence it represented. But most importantly I think of why it came to be in my hands, and the remorse it carries. Eddy died in the area of Hoc Mon, where the Vietnamese boy had been born. There the two young men came together in battle on March 4th, 1968. I know about this Viet Cong soldier who survived, who may have been the one who killed Eddy, because of Jim. If it weren't for Jim, I wouldn't be opening this box or writing this story.

I met Jim Petersen in June of 1968, three months after Eddy was killed. He never knew Eddy but heard a lot about him because I was grieving, as was my family. I married Jim in 1971 and although we divorced three years later, we remained friends. In 2009, he called to say he was heading to Vietnam. After retiring from the Marines as a pilot, then, after working as a Coast Guard pilot, and then after retiring from his third career as an airline pilot, he began an international environmental consulting business called Listen to the Earth, which was taking him to Vietnam for consultation.

Sometimes I wonder about the timing of events and think it's not by chance that we had recently met with Andy Wahrenbrock and learned the details and exact location of Eddy's death. So I asked Jim if he would take a picture of the village of Hoc Mon if he were to drive past that area. I shared with him all we had learned from Andy.

Jim was driving through Vietnam with Vietnamese government officials from Ho Chi Minh City (Saigon). They came to Hoc Mon and Jim asked if they would stop the car so that he could walk around this village. He had forgotten his camera, but wanted to check out the village, feeling like it was hallowed ground, the exact location of Eddy's last moments. Jim clearly stood out, a 6'4", Caucasian, blonde American walking through their little village where most were darker skinned and much shorter. Villagers began to follow him until there was an entourage of people surrounding them. The government men acted as translators so Jim could converse with them. Jim eventually encountered a group of weathered-looking Viet Cong veterans.

Jim tells them through the translators that he stopped at this village because his friend's uncle was killed there and he told them the date of the battle.

Several of the men say they were in that battle on that day. They knew this because it was their home village and it was uncommon for a large battle to be fought there. They tell their story: they saw the American soldiers coming across the bridge toward the village, so they laid in wait, hiding within the walls of the deserted huts. When American troops arrived close to the village, they opened fire. Jim told the veterans about Eddy getting killed immediately. One man began to cry silently, tears slipping down his face. He then told of his losses, of his years spent in tunnels fighting against overwhelming odds, and of his comrade-in-arms, a woman he had hoped to marry, whom he had witnessed disappear before his eyes in a hail of body parts when a bomb was dropped from a B-52, from 20,000 feet above. He told of other family members killed—women, children, the elderly. His eyes brimmed with tears as he told of his losses. He had been a young man who had only known war his entire life; a young man who wanted freedom for his country, who wanted to live in peace, who wanted the French gone, the Americans gone. He fought what he called "The American War" because he had no choice. Most of his comrades didn't survive. Jim said you could almost witness the events as you looked into his weary eyes. When they finished their conversation, and Jim was about to leave, this aging veteran pleaded, "Please wait while I get something. I have something for your friend."

Jim watched him pedal away on his bicycle and he told me later that the moment turned into twenty minutes. He was beginning to wonder if the fellow would ever return. Finally, he spotted him pedaling along the dirt road, a cloud of red dust encircling him. When he approached Jim, he got off his bike and handed him what I now hold in my hands. "Give this to your friend," he said.

Eventually, Jim called to say he had something for me from Vietnam and that it had to do with Eddy but he wouldn't tell me what it was until he could bring it. I couldn't imagine what it could be, and I anxiously waited. Finally, after a *year*, I told him I couldn't wait any longer, and he needed to tell me. So, he told me and mailed it.

I hold the box to my heart, knowing what's inside. It isn't so much what's in it, but that it was a gift from the enemy, a gift from a Viet Cong soldier who may have been the one to kill Eddy. For forty years the word Viet Cong held negative feelings, made me shudder. How could it not? They killed Eddy. And now, a gift, something in a little metal box, from the enemy. I put the box on the table in front of me. I touch one end of the red ribbon and pull. I lift off the lid of the metal box and there it is—neatly folded, fitting the inner space like a pea fills a pod. I'm in awe of what I'm about to see. I gently lift it out. It's folded into a small, fat rectangle. I open it up to see the orange, blue and yellow Viet Cong battle flag that was flying at the scene of Eddy's death, the flag that the boy had revered, the flag that represented all that he had fought for. Jim told me that he had to wash the blood out of it because he didn't want me to see it that way. Though it still holds the smell of blood in its cloth, it carries the message of remorse.

This battle-scarred man, whose name I do not know, offered the flag he had cherished for forty years, as if he had reached into himself, pulled out his heart and offered his amends with outstretched hands to a family he had never met. This aging veteran of a war he didn't choose, a war he abhorred, a war that killed his loved ones, reached out his arms to the family of his enemy, reached with a gift, the only gift that could matter, a gift that survived time and distance, the offering of his battle flag, the symbol of his country, his honor, his duty. A peace offering, an absolution.

The Viet Cong veteran's gift of his battle flag, held by U.S. Army veterans who fought against him on March 4th, 1968, in Hoc Mon, Vietnam, where and when Eddy lost his life. Left to right: Jerry Miller, Jerry Counts, Andy Wahrenbrock, Dave Glass.

Chapter Twenty-Six
On the Bank of Stenner Creek
California
1968–Present Day

The cookies I sent Eddy returned, a month after he was killed. The coffee can looked like it had been through war, as it was mangled and squished, looking the way I felt.

Every morning at my college there was a moment when everyone stood wherever they were to listen to *The Star Spangled Banner*, and to look at the American flag that flew in the center of an open area. I stood quietly, and listened, but in my youthful resentfulness, at eighteen, I couldn't look at the flag. I felt angry that Eddy wasn't here on this campus going to school like he should be, angry at our government who forced Eddy to go to war and be killed so that South Vietnam would not become communist. Despite the politics and uselessness of that war, Eddy died a hero, of noble character, because he did what he was called to do without one word of complaint. This time, instead of pretending he was the good cowboy at the movies like when we were kids, he was, for certain, in real life, the good cowboy.

At Cuesta College, Eddy's wrestling coach, Warren Hansen, started a coach's award in Eddy's name, awarded to the most dedicated, hardest working and coachable team member. The award continued for a while until Coach Hansen took another position and the award in

Eddy's name fell away because the newer coaches hadn't known him. After forty-five years, Coach Hansen contacted my sister, Karen, from her posting on the online Virtual Wall (www. virtualwall.org), and wrote, "I just wanted to say to you that Ed was a great young man and I was sorry to see him leave school and very saddened when I heard that he had been killed in action. He was one of my favorite students/athletes, always clean cut, respectful, hardworking, friendly and overall just very likeable." In a later correspondence, he wrote, "I can certainly see that your family truly loved Ed as I did also. He was one of the few athletes present during those early start up years at Cuesta that I would have been proud to call my son."

The farm might be gone, and Eddy might be gone, but the Zion Lutheran Church still remains on the corner of Foothill and Santa Rosa Street. Inside its warm interior there is a sanctuary light in Eddy's honor, in remembrance of the boy who lived nearby, who made ranches in the dirt, and grew dreams in his heart.

Maryanne eventually married someone she met in college and they stayed in that eastern state while raising two children. After their children were grown, they returned to San Luis Obispo.

Grandpa took Arthur to where Eddy's forty or fifty sheep were, and told him to choose all that he wanted. Arthur picked up where Eddy left off, raising and showing sheep at the fair.

Grandpa gave the Mercedes to me, Judy and Mom to share. Every time I sat in that car I thought of it as Eddy's and the sadness engulfed me. He used some of the

Army death benefit money to buy Sandy a Volvo wagon that she still drives today.

Grandpa used much of the Army death benefit money to buy land in the country where he could raise a couple of steer and grow hay. He eventually built a house on the property where he and Grandma moved to.

I didn't see how Grandma and Grandpa could survive this loss of the second of their children to die a violent death. First Erma, then Eddy. Grandpa didn't live too many years after Eddy. He died six years later of cancer, and six months after moving into their new home in the country. Maybe it was brought on by stress from this heart-wrenching tragedy of losing his little shadow, his "Daddy's Tail."

My cousin John says Eddy's death profoundly changed his life. He had joined FFA in San Jose to be like Eddy. He wanted to move back to San Luis Obispo after high school to become a rancher along with Eddy. Instead he gave up that idea and stayed in San Jose.

Andy Wahrenbrock, in 2002-2003, spearheaded a plan to build a memorial in Kern County, California. He chaired the Kern Veteran's Memorial Foundation board and after years of fundraising, the memorial was completed and dedicated in downtown Bakersfield in 2007. An additional Wall of Valor was dedicated in 2011. For Andy, this memorial represents a promise to remember those who gave the ultimate sacrifice for our country.

On Veteran's Day, 2011, Andy traveled to the Vietnam Memorial in Washington D.C. On the ground below the names of Edward August Schultz and Lorence Marion Lundby, he left a bronze plaque that he'd had engraved with his words:

"Einstein once said that God does not play dice
Those of us who have walked into the ambush kill zone know
That in the minutes after the first shot rings out
God and the Devil himself do"

–Andrew Wahrenbrock
2/12-25th Inf 1968

Jerry Counts returned to Texas, at age twenty-one, after his year in Vietnam. He'd lived a year in hell and said he was never leaving Texas again. However, twenty-five years after the war ended, their platoon began to have reunions in different parts of the country. In July 2012, they met in Ruidoso, New Mexico, and I was blessed to join them. My daughter, Lauren, my second child of three, went with me. I was in awe of meeting these men whom I thought had died in a land mine. I took videos, listened to their stories, looked at their albums and pictures and felt their pain and what this war did to them. I met with Andy, Dave Glass, Jerry Miller and Jerry Counts. Robert Coulter had planned to be there but had to cancel due to a sudden family tragedy. Jerry Counts told of his tears as he dragged Eddy and Larry's bodies to the evacuation helicopter when he was just twenty years old. After I got home, I sent him a miniature book of Bible verses that Eddy had kept dear to his heart.

Though Eddy didn't live long enough to have

children, traces of him live on. Flashes and glimmers show up in his nieces, nephews and great nieces and nephews. My brother, Arthur, raised sheep throughout high school, and became FFA president. My second daughter carries his middle name as her middle name: Lauren August. My oldest daughter, Lindsey, reminded me of him from the time she could talk—she begged for a horse, begged to do the fair, became FFA President, earned the State Farmer award, was on the parliamentary procedure team like he was, showed heifers and steer, even worked at Madonna Inn, where he had worked. He would be proud to know that his great niece, who followed in his footsteps without ever knowing him, is now an agribusiness professor at Cal Poly. My son, Michael, has Eddy's same character traits of kind-heartedness, honesty and work ethic and ranks doing the right thing as priority. Sandy named one of her sons Eddy and his daughter also has the middle name of August. Sandy sees traits of Eddy in most of her six children—in the flash of a smile, a look in the eye. Interestingly, the one with his name reminds her of him the most. This Eddy has his Uncle Eddy's smile, as does my daughter, Lindsey. Sandy's son, Sal, has a son, Joaquin, born on my birthday a few years ago, and every time I saw him as a baby, I saw his resemblance to Eddy's baby pictures. My cousin, Linda, has a son named Darren, who is a farmer with farming in his blood, and Linda adds that he has the same long eyelashes, beautiful eyes and similar charming smile of his great uncle whom he never knew.

During my lifetime, I've sometimes looked at Erma's photograph and wondered who she was. Now, I gaze at the photograph I took of Eddy on Christmas, a week before he left and it's different than when I look at Erma's picture. Both died tragically, both died young, but I look at Eddy and see my friend, my playmate, my schoolmate, my uncle who was more like a brother, and the memories flood back. It must be what my mother felt when she looked at pictures of Erma. In this photo, he's at the head of the table, and the adults in our family line its sides. Eddy's elbow is propped on the table and his chin rests in his hand. He stares directly into the camera as I shoot the picture. Nobody else is looking. I don't care because the picture of him is what I wanted. He's looking with those eyes, those quiet, knowing eyes. I ask myself, does he know in that moment that he won't come back.

In one of his final letters from Vietnam, written to Maryanne, Eddy wrote: *I feel closer to God than I ever have before.* And with that, as I hold the flag of the enemy,

I realize that hatred and love, grief and healing seem at variance, seem in opposition, yet they are on the same spectrum called love, and I know that I must forgive.

I look into his face in that picture, the face in that moment in time, into the past, and I say, "Eddy, you saved my life once on the bank of Stenner Creek. If only your rules could work. If only I could count to ten and you would come back to life, like you did that day in your chaps, your cowboy boots and your black hat that flopped from side to side, when you galloped around the tank house on your imaginary horse, with a smile on your face and joy in your heart."

In Remembrance

58,267 U.S. soldiers were killed in Vietnam
39,996 were 22 years old or younger
8,283 were 19 years old
3,103 were 18 years old
12 were 17 years old
5 were 16 years old
1 was 15 years old
997 were killed on their first day there
1,448 were killed on their last day there
31 sets of brothers were killed
Three sets of fathers and sons were killed
The most deaths for a single day was January 31, 1968—245 deaths
The most deaths for a single month was May 1968—2,415 deaths
ARVN (Army of the Republic of Vietnam) had about 266,000 deaths
1,100,000 North Vietnamese Army and Viet Cong military personnel were killed

Grandma, my mom, Judy and I visited the travelling wall; also remembering Eddy was David Stafford (right) who rode the bus with Eddy to the Induction Center; circa, 1998.

Resources

Books

Boyle, Charles J. *Absolution*. Spotsylvania, VA: Sergeant Kirkland's Press, 1999.
Drury, Bob and Clavin, Tom. *Last Man Out*. New York: Free Press, 2011.
Marlantes, Karl. *Matterhorn*. New York: Grove Press, 2010.
Van Devanter, Lynda. *Home Before Morning*. New York: Beaufont Books, Inc., 1983

Internet

www.about.com
www.bbc.com/onthisday
www.history.com
www.militaryfactory.com
www.212warriors.com
www.wikipedia.org

Online Memorials

www.thewall-usa.com
www.virtualwall.org
www.vvmf.org

Movies and DVDs

Platoon. (motion picture).Director: Oliver Stone, 1986.
We Were Soldiers. (motion picture). Director: Randall Wallace, 2002.
Vietnam in HD. (DVD). The History Channel. 2011.
The Vietnam War. (DVD). The History Channel. 2008.

Charities

Worthy veteran charities to donate to (who spend at least 75% of their budget on their cause) taken from www.charitywatch.org:

Armed Services YMCA of the USA
Bob Woodruff Family Foundation
Fisher House Foundation
Guide Dog Foundation for the Blind
Homes for our Troops
Injured Marine Semper Fi Fund
Intrepid Fallen Heroes Fund
National Military Family Association
Operation Homefront
Tragedy Assistance Program for Survivors

And:
Edward August Schultz Scholarship Fund
https://www.youcaring.com/students-who-lost-a-parent-in-any-war-or-ffa-students-469329 (youcaring charges a 2.9% fee; otherwise all of donation goes toward this fund)

Made in the USA
Charleston, SC
04 October 2016